Praise for *Tarot for the Hard Work*

"An important and profoundly edifying book for all tarot readers. We want to be antiracist and dismantle internalized racism, but how? *Tarot for the Hard Work* provides actionable exercises in addition to being a workbook for self-reflection. This is meditation and liberation work keyed to the Major Arcana set on a path of healing. Perhaps the most important tarot text that will define this decade. Maria Minnis exudes compassion and wisdom."

—**Benebell Wen, author of** *Holistic Tarot*

"Maria Minnis delivers a punch to the gut with Tarot for the Hard Work. It's a refreshing, courageous take on using tarot as more than a reflective tool but also as a spark for tangible societal shifts. This book confronts the intricate issues of racism directly, charting a course for both personal enlightenment and community action through the Major Arcana. Minnis embraces the tough conversations and ushers the reader toward a voyage of self-exploration that's as illuminating as it is actionable. It's a stirring read—raw and perceptive—that not only provokes deep introspection but also arms the reader with a practical blueprint to actively dismantle prejudice. For anyone dedicated to combating racism and seeking a uniquely inspiring approach, Minnis's work is a crucial addition to your arsenal."

—**Mat Auryn, author of** *Psychic Witch* **and** *Mastering Magick*

"The world is changing and so is tarot. Back in the day, tarot was associated with divination, but now it's taking us in a whole new direction. In *Tarot for the Hard Work*, author Maria Minnis helps the reader open up the Fool's bag to unpack their privilege so they can show up and fight for an equitable world using the twenty-two Major Arcana cards. Magic rituals, affirmations, and tarot interpretations sit side by side with suggestions for effective, everyday actions for combatting systemic racism and oppression. This is a must-have book for tarot readers and anyone who wants a just, equitable, and sustainable world."

—**Theresa Reed, author of** *The Cards You're Dealt*

T0001026

"Since the very first time I read Maria Minnis's work, I have been waiting impatiently for a book, knowing that it was only a matter of time. And as high as my hopes were for *Tarot for the Hard Work*, this book still managed to blow me away. Minnis is the real deal. From transformative perspectives on tarot archetypes to clever action items for every kind of reader and activist, *Tarot for the Hard Work* doesn't apologize for being exactly what it is: a brilliant primer and essential guide for utilizing tarot's truth in personal and collective antiracism work. Not only did I learn something new about the tarot on every page, but I found myself challenged, inspired, and energized too. This book is a must-read for every tarot reader, as well as anyone who is serious about engaging with antiracism work but isn't sure where to start. I can't recommend this book highly enough."

—**Meg Jones Wall, author of** *Finding the Fool*

"Tarot is a tool of awakening, and *Tarot for the Hard Work* takes that seriously, challenging us to truly awaken to the internalized racism and structures of white supremacy that live inside of us, no matter how 'woke' we think we are. This book is an antidote to the watered-down 'love and light' tarot treatment—a tender and supportive guide to self-exploration and reclamation, a rallying cry to create better futures, and a practical toolkit for action and change. It's also an excellent tarot book, one that not only provides progressive explorations of the cards but bridges that into embodiment and real-world action. It's often said that using tarot will change your life. *Tarot for the Hard Work* won't just change your life; it can help us change the world."

—**Charlie Claire Burgess, author of** *Radical Tarot* **and** *Fifth Spirit Tarot*

"Tarot can struggle in the liminal space between the spiritual and the practical, but Maria Minnis powerfully tosses it over the abyss and plants it firmly in earthly soil, asking profound and necessary questions that each of us—but especially white people—need to engage with in order to address the long-standing, systemic racism that permeates our white-dominant culture. She compassionately and thoroughly weaves tarot archetypes and correspondences into the web of intersectional liberation, highlighting the interconnectedness of causes like climate and disability justice with anti-Blackness and inviting everyone to go deeper into their own radical efforts.

"*Tarot For the Hard Work* is not only a resource itself, but a collection of resources, offering additional reading materials, voices to listen to, ideas to germinate on, historical and present-day information to research and learn, and tangible ways to put this work into action in your community. With this incredible book in your hands, there are no excuses as to why you cannot engage with antiracism in every aspect of your life. These pages will change you, if you let them."

—Rebecca Scolnick, author of *The Witch's Book of Numbers*

"*Tarot for the Hard Work* is a beautiful examination of tarot through the ever-important lens of antiracism. Maria Minnis makes our mission clear as we develop new understandings of the cards based on her writing, research, and activities that make this whole process feel fun and hopeful in this seminal work. Maria Minnis is the future of tarot, and I believe that with my whole heart. *Tarot for the Hard Work* is the book we need right now."

—Cassandra Snow, author of *Queering the Tarot*

"Author Maria Minnis shows us that the archetypes of the Major Arcana can be put to far more significant use than kept as mere tools for fortune-telling. Under her firm and insightful direction, they become a series of foundation blocks: jumping-off points to help us create a personalized toolbox that will—if we do the hard work—transform each of us into confident and useful advocates for others who face discrimination."

—Alison Cross, former chair of The Tarot Association
of the British Isles (TABI) and author of
A Year In the Wildwood, Tarot Court Card DNA, and *Tarot Kaizen*

"*Tarot for the Hard Work* is a necessary read for any tarot reader. Minnis has perfectly captured both the difficulty that comes from confronting internalized racism as well as the absolute joy we can find in building a more just world. This book feels so fresh, showing us a side of these archetypes that we desperately need to meet."

—Siri Vincent Plouff, coauthor of *Lessons from the Empress*

"In *Tarot for the Hard Work*, Maria uses the tarot archetypes as a tool for relearning and confronting racism in a constructive, healing way, showing you how to tap into your magic to make change happen. With practical and easy-to-do exercises, wonderful book recommendations, and empowering affirmations, *Tarot for the Hard Work* will move your moral compass in a healthier and more enlightened way."

—**Jen Sankey, author of *Stardust Wanderer Tarot***

"*Tarot for the Hard Work* is an excellent guide to understanding how the Major Arcana archetypes of the tarot deck show up in our lives and how we can work within them to bring about social change. Maria Minnis brings her deep knowledge of the history of tarot into the present, offering exceptionally sharp insight into how these cards can help us see ourselves and our world more clearly today in order to work toward a better tomorrow for all. Through examples, exercises, affirmations, keywords, and more, Minnis opens a practical path for building a more equitable world through the hard work of self-discovery and altering our consciousness. Her forward-thinking belief in humanity infuses every page. This book is not a prescription for behavioral change; it is an invitation to evolution."

—**Melinda Lee Holm, author of *Your Tarot Guide***

"Of the many ways that tarot can be used, perhaps none is more important than knowing how to work with the cards to do the hard work of confronting and healing our own biases and prejudices, as well as the biases and prejudices that we have inherited from our familial lines and our culture at large. We owe a great deal of thanks to gifted reader and writer Maria Minnis for opening the road to working with the cards in this manner. As she states, it is hard work but it is also the best kind of work, work that can truly create more freedom—for ourselves and others."

—**Briana Saussy, author of *Making Magic* and *Star Child***

"This book should be on everyone's bookshelf, not just tarot readers. EVERYONE. In *Tarot for the Hard Work*, author Maria Minnis helps awaken us to our truest, bravest, most compassionate selves. It's a luminous work of love. Minnis shines a torch illuminating our path toward justice. This author knows that her readers don't need to be coddled; we need to be reminded that we have the power to create a more beautiful, loving world. When we look through her lens, tarot can help us get there. Possibilities for what tarot can do in our lives— and in the world—expand. The meanings of the cards grow more luscious and rich. I honestly don't think I could go back to the tarot I knew before this book came to me. I wouldn't want to. Minnis breathes new life into this ancient art. Not only is her book a pleasure to read, it's a treat to work with and an honor to have as teacher and guide. Compulsory reading for anyone interested in personal and collective liberation."

—**Amanda Yates Garcia, author of** *Initiated* **and host of the** *Between the Worlds* **podcast**

"All of the most important work we do in our lives is ongoing and never complete. I could say that Maria Minnis's groundbreaking and urgently necessary book is the one that I wish I had when I started unlearning anti-Blackness over twenty years ago, and that would be true; but instead, I'm so grateful that it's the one I have to guide me now."

—**Lane Smith, author of** *Seventy-Eight Acts of Liberation: Tarot to Transform Our World*

TAROT
FOR THE HARD
WORK

an Archetypal Journey to Confront Racism
and Inspire Collective Healing

MARIA MINNIS

FOREWORD BY RASHUNDA TRAMBLE

WEISER
BOOKS

To the witches who do something when they see something. Every one of your lives is a divine spell. I don't have to wonder what would happen if we tried to change the world, because I see the evidence all around me.

This edition first published in 2024 by Weiser Books, an imprint of
Red Wheel/Weiser, LLC
With offices at: 65 Parker Street, Suite 7, Newburyport, MA 01950
www.redwheelweiser.com

ISBN: 978-1-57863-807-9
Library of Congress Cataloging-in-Publication Data

Names: Minnis, Maria, 1990- author. Title: Tarot for the hard work : an archetypal journey to confront racism and inspire collective healing / Maria Minnis ; foreword by Rashunda Tramble. Description: Newburyport, MA : Weiser Books, 2023. | Includes bibliographical references. | Summary: "A provocative exploration of the 22 Major Arcana that re-envisions these archetypes as beacons that illuminate the various ways racisms takes root-both in ourselves and in the world-and how these insights can be turned into self-awareness, self-love, and positive social action"-- Provided by publisher.
Identifiers: LCCN 2023037494 | ISBN 9781578638079 (trade paperback) | ISBN 9781633413085 (ebook) Subjects: LCSH: Major arcana (Tarot) | Anti-racism--Miscellanea. | BISAC: BODY, MIND & SPIRIT / Divination / Tarot | SELF-HELP / Spiritual Classification: LCC BF1879.T2 M573 2023 | DDC 133.3/2424--dc23/eng/20231011
LC record available at https://lccn.loc.gov/2023037494

Cover and interior design by Sky Peck Design
Typeset in Arno Pro

Printed in the United States of America
IBI

10 9 8 7 6 5 4 3 2 1

CONTENTS

ACKNOWLEDGMENTS

Sitting in the back corner of a coffee shop in western Virginia, I planted a seed that flourished into this project. I'd been aware of white supremacy and its manifestations since childhood. (Imagine, a nine-year-old with opinions about cop culture!) But the rapid proliferation of publicly documented racial abuse and increasing confidence of bigots and their sycophants bewildered me. I didn't know what to do. I was still acutely traumatized by what I saw, heard, and physically felt counterprotesting at the 2017 Unite the Right rally. The few antiracism groups in my area focused heavily on training white people to be antiracist. Overwhelmed, I turned to a familiar structure: tarot.

Inspired by various tarot archetypes, I filled a notebook with realistic every-day actions I could take to combat racism, internally and out in the world. The notebook turned into a blog that morphed into this book. This section lists some of the brilliant people and places that helped make it happen. I'm aware that I'm ridiculously effusive (note my natal Venus in Cancer in the third house), so I've tried to be brief. However, my brevity is unreflective of how dearly I adore and respect them.

Stephen: Thank you for building a dream life with me. When wake up and journal in the morning, I am awestricken that every day is always happier than the last. My eyes have never been wider, my curiosity never more active. Without question, I'd endure everything again just to get to you. This book is threaded with your love, encouragement, levity, and intellect. Thank you for everything, including sharing the Tardis with me to complete this project. Loving is hard for most people, but we're not most people. I love you and will find you in every lifetime, dimension, and matrix.

Mom, Dad, Denzel, Grandma Rachel, Grandma Audrey, Aunt Deanna, Uncle Afi, and my benevolent ancestors: I could not begin to list all the ways you've shaped the kind, curious, and silly person I am today. There's nothing I could do to pay you back for believing in me. Thank you for teaching me, feeding me, sharing laughs, encouraging and celebrating my ambition, playing with me, and giving me advice based on your lived experiences. Most of all, thank you for loving me unconditionally. I love you all!

Hilary: You are my sister for eternity. Come to my bosom. Since we were kids, I knew there was a kinship between us. And there surely is. The world is not always kind to sensitive lasses like us, but we've got each other. Your generous love is deep, gentle, tender, magical, trustworthy, and otherworldly. It's actually inexplicable, but those words are the best I've got. Never forget how fiercely I love you.

Sea: I could not have saved my own life without your love, care, and guidance. There is no one on this planet quite like you. I know I "did the work," but you were the one who showed me that true liberation was possible. You held my hand through it all and beyond. I could not have written this book the way I needed to without you. I love you, eternally.

Andi B.: I've always had a piece of my heart just for you—I just didn't know it until you radiated into my life. Real recognizes real, and I recognize you. Whether we're trying to walk down a million steps or having heart-to-hearts on the playa, you amaze me. Thank you for helping me rediscover and love myself. Thank you for helping me feel joy again. I didn't believe I deserved friends until I met you. And now you're family. I love you, for real and forever.

Lynn C.: How lovely is it that we found each other? How lovely was our timing, to grow close while enduring massive parallel life shifts? How lovely are you? It is impossible to describe. Find my love when you touch a gardenia petal, sniff a magnolia blossom, or find an interesting insect. Growing alongside you, someone I love beyond articulation, is one of the great joys of my life.

Amanda Y. G.: Friend, I love you so much. I witness your depth, wisdom, and extensive knowledge, and I smile. How could I not? You helped me accept that, yes, I am a powerful witch. My magic is forever imbued with your inspiration. Thank you for helping me share my work with the world. Without you, this book could never have existed the way I wanted it to.

Cassandra Snow: Because of you, my #1 bucket list item of becoming a published author came true! You saw my potential, asked if I'd considered writing a book, and gave me the confidence to draft a proposal. Then you connected me to the lovely people at Red Wheel/Weiser. Thank you for helping me realize my childhood dream. I will always be grateful.

Kathryn Sky-Peck: You are the definition of the word advocate. Thank you so, so much for supporting this project, always keeping it real with me, and being receptive to my ideas and opinions. I could not value your guidance any more.

Rashunda Tramble: When people say I'm a "tarot reader's tarot reader," I give them a look and respond, "Umm . . . have you ever worked with Rashunda?" Thank you for being my tarot reader, teacher, and foreword writer. Thank you also for sharing your brilliance, many talents, and tremendous intelligence with the world. I sure wouldn't mind a world with more people like you!

Cammie Krise: It's impossible for me to articulate how much I appreciate you. Thank you for noticing something special in a shy, bookish five-year-old. You helped my mom and me in immeasurable ways that set me up to thrive. Without a doubt, I know that your generous spirit and sweet smile make the world a brighter place.

My darling friends: When I sat down and wrote a list of all my friends, I was simultaneously astonished and beaming with joy. I went from forced isolation to having tons of affectionate friends I never have to mask around. The following list is far from comprehensive, but I wanted to name a few people who helped me liberate myself from the shackles of abuse and get free. I offer deep bows of gratitude to Anita M., Bree K., Imani D., Jasper J., Lynn C., Marissa K., Lane S., and Sarah AA. You saved my life.

Rancho crew: Thank you for accepting me into an enchanted community in which I can be wild and vulnerable. I've always wanted to have a big friend family, but I never imagined how much love I could feel within one. Wow.

My radical witch community: You know who you are. Changemakers, you are constantly expanding perceptions of tarot and witchcraft in unprecedented ways, and I am so honored to be part of this work. Thank you for elevating my work and creating more inclusive magical spaces that get more and more people to realize the magic in themselves.

Sarah Faith Gottesdiener: I can't thank you enough for the powerful and energizing reading that inspired me to start the Antiracism with the Tarot blog. With this and so much more, you have profoundly changed my life. Helping copyedit the Many Moons planner the past few years has felt liberating, expansive, and deeply meaningful. I will miss working with you and Maddie—you two are rock stars! Love and respect you, for real.

To my students and clients: My work is powered by your loving presence and curiosity. Thank you for sharing space with me and the honor of being invited into your lives. I learn something new every time I interact with you.

To the people of my ideological lineage: I also want to thank some of the people whose offerings to the world have informed, shaped, and influenced my work in ways immeasurable: Angeles Arrien, Melody Beattie, Benazir Bhutto, Björk, Rabbi Mychal Copeland, Pema Chödrön, Dorothy Dandridge, Rebekah Erev, Marvin Gaye, Nikki Giovanni, Fannie Lou Hamer, Jill Hammer, Thich Nhat Hanh, Abraham Heschel, bell hooks, Marsha P. Johnson, June Jordan, Søren Kierkegaard, Ketzirah Lesser, Pixie Lighthorse, Audre Lorde, Maimonides, Dori Midnight, Toni Morrison, Zora Neale Hurston, Bree Newsome, OutKast, Rachel Pollack, Rainer Maria Rilke, Rick Rubin, Rabbi Yoni Regev, Betye Saar, Sade, Buffy Sainte-Marie, Nina Simone, Luisah Teish, Meg Jones Wall, Tammy Wynette, Malcolm X, Venus X, and Yoko Ono. Thank you.

To the Shekinah: I witness your presence everywhere I go and in all my visions of a future that is more loving, accessible, equitable, community-driven, and custodial to this planet. The world to come is the world that is coming, and you remind me every single day. תודה על הכל. אכבד אותך עד קץ הימים!

This book was written on the lands of the Monacan, Ohlone, Ramaytush, Muwekma, Tongva, Chumash, and Fernandeño Tataviam peoples. Thank you for your stewardship and wisdom. It's "Land back!" until it's all back.

FOREWORD

As I write these words, Jordan Neely's body is lying in a casket in a Harlem church. Neely, a thirty-year-old Black man known for performing impersonations of Michael Jackson in Times Square, was killed by a white U.S. Marine veteran who put him in a chokehold on a New York City subway. He did this in order to "protect" the other passengers. What did they so drastically need protection from? Someone who was homeless, thirsty, and having a mental health crisis. And of the multitudes of mentally ill, homeless New Yorkers who make underground public transportation their home, Jordan Neely was an obvious, outstanding, especially scary threat: he was a Black man.

A clip of the murder made the social media rounds, as is the macabre norm now. You may have seen it. You may have even become outraged and retweeted it. But I have a question for you: what did you do after? And by the time this book lands in your hands, there will probably be another hashtaggable Black victim of someone who took the law into theirs. What will you do then? My friend, I ask this question not to offend, or even provoke. I ask because I'm genuinely curious. I wonder if you've ever considered or observed your reaction when news of yet another unarmed person of color being killed or seriously injured for walking, driving, riding a bike, sitting in a car, or, hell, breathing, reaches your eyes, ears or device. Does that reaction morph into action? And can that action, possibly, maybe be one tiny step towards healing our deep racial wounds?

But healing racial wounds isn't only about the murder of Black people. Let's take a look at Black mental and physical health. In the series "From Birth to Death,"* the Associated Press explores the effects of racism on the health of Black Americans, investigating the inequities that Black people face in the medical system on a daily basis. According to the AP, 14.8 percent of Black babies born in

---

* Kat Stafford, Annie Ma, and Aaron Morrison, "Project Home: From Birth to Death," a digital presentation, Associated Press, n.d., https://apnews.com/article/from-birth-to-death-series-2b2f56844fe6f309be541b45aef2e281.

2021 were premature, more than any other ethnic group. And Black people are almost three times as likely to die during pregnancy or childbirth than any other race. Some 18 percent of Black youth "said they were exposed to racial trauma often or very often in their life" with 50 percent saying that they experience moderate to severe symptoms of depression. The AP continues, revealing that Black teens "report experiencing an average of five instances of racial discrimination per day" and that between 1991 and 2019 they had the highest increase in suicide attempts compared to their peers of other races: 80 percent. That's right, an 80 percent *increase*. The news organization posits that these horrifying statistics are the result of medical racism, one of the many offspring white supremacy has birthed into the world. But this information, as shocking as it is, should come as no surprise.

I have to be honest here. As someone born and raised in the Deep South, with my DNA stitched together by the thread of slavery, I laugh when anyone suggests that systemic racism can be healed. Systemic racism is what "made America great" and why so many on the wrong side of history want to make it "great" again, on their terms, using updated methods proudly inherited from their foremothers and forefathers. But as I laugh, there's a tiny part of me that wants to believe; I want to believe that there are good people out there who want to drive a stake in the heart of systemic racism. I want to believe that there are good people out there who want to pound that stake even deeper, pushing it through the many layers of systemic racism: misogyny, transphobia, homophobia, xenophobia, classism, and white supremacy. And I want to believe that there are good people in the spiritual community who want to do something, *anything*, but just don't know what or how. Yes, sometimes the laugh gets louder, and even more amplified by my roots. I'm from Memphis, the city where Dr. King was killed by a white man's bullet, and where fifty-five years later Tyre Nichols was killed by a Black cop's baton. But that tiny part keeps going, keeps trying to drown out the laughter while still believing that good people exist—good people who know in their hearts that racism can be defeated with the right tools. That tiny part, as small as it is, is mighty. And that tiny part believes in you.

Yes, you're one of those good people I believe in. Why? Well, first, we have something in common: a love of tarot. Both you and I believe that tarot isn't just for fortune telling. It can also help us discover what influences our thoughts and actions. Which archetypes, numbers, symbols activate something deep in the core of our being? We believe that tarot helps us access and analyze hidden messages, imprints, and signals we've picked up by living in this society. Tarot allows us to address these issues. Tarot is a catalyst for change.

Second, you're reading this book. *Tarot for the Hard Work* is not for the faint of heart. As Maria Minnis states, this book "is a tool for passionately demolishing structural oppression. It is a tool for white people who want to use their privilege for mass liberation. It is a tool for Black and Brown people living in a structurally racist society that's intent on selling self-hatred and shame to marginalized people and making money off their backs." Both you and I want to—and must—use any and all tools we have at our disposal to crack the foundation of racism. *Tarot for the Hard Work* is just one of those tools.

Think of this book as a map that we can take with us on a voyage as we discover our personal, subliminal views on race and how we're impacted. Each card of the Major Arcana serves as a waypoint that challenges us to rethink our views on racial equity. Starting with the Fool, Minnis asks us to embrace the unknown and open ourselves to the creativity we need for social justice work. Then Minnis takes our hand, leading us along a path towards the World and the liberation that follows. No stone is left unturned. Topics such as protecting public spaces, the impact of climate change on BIPOCs, and expanding health care are carefully and logically linked to the cards. Minnis offers keywords, exercises, and journal prompts, providing real, actionable tarot-based steps to bring us closer to understanding our role in dismantling racist systems by using progressive definitions of the Major Arcana archetypes—not as set characters in someone else's story, but as fluid ones in ours. In addition, she tackles the "love and lighting" of spirituality that blocks us from addressing the pertinent issues affecting both the magical and mundane worlds. Minnis leads us to and through this somewhat uncomfortable, but fully rewarding, process, all the while encouraging us to stretch, grow, and become aware.

Tarot for the Hard Work asks us to set aside our standard operating procedures when it comes to race, no matter our background, no matter how "woke" we assume ourselves to be. It encourages us to think of the issues within the framework of tarot and then expand those thoughts and insights into the real world and, most importantly, act upon them. *Tarot for the Hard Work* endeavors to show that a tarot deck isn't a sign of spiritual enlightenment. Rather, it is a work permit.

Can seventy-eight pieces of cardstock counter four hundred years of racial injustice? No. But we can add them to our toolkits. We can use them to look deep inside ourselves, acknowledge the role we have, and then use that energy of acknowledgment as fuel for action. This work may give you pause. Some of the statements, questions, and exercises in *Tarot for the Hard Work* may require you to set your preconceived notions of who you are aside. By the time you finish this book, you may even want to leave those notions where they are.

I asked earlier what you would do if—or let's be honest *when*—another Black or Brown person is robbed of their life and humanity and reduced to a tweetable hashtag. You probably didn't have an answer. And that's okay. Actually, not having an answer is probably the "right" answer. Not knowing and being open are the epitome of Fool's energy. And that energy, the energy of curiosity and a willingness to learn, will be more than enough to sustain you through the hard work.

Let's begin.

—Rashunda Tramble of Stay Woke Tarot
Coauthor of *The Numinous Tarot Guide: A New Way to Read the Cards*

INTRODUCTION

We begin with the premise that tarot is a tool of self-discovery. The cards provide us a tactile means to do inner work and grow as individuals, to unveil our "true" selves. In particular, the twenty-two cards of the Major Arcana depict "the grand picture"—classically they represent the archetypal energies we all share within the great universal unconscious. Our vivid trek through the majors has been described as the "hero's journey" and the "great work." It's an alchemical process by which we move from innocence to knowledge, from unconsciousness to consciousness.

In other words, the majors present us with opportunities to move from ignorance, denial, and complacency to awareness, responsibility, and action. We might say that the journey wakes us up.

Tarot for the Hard Work is a potent partner for this journey. It is an array of Major Arcana writings and exercises for untangling racism, both externally and internally.

The word "racism" is tossed around so often that we don't always consider what it really means, what it actually entails. Ask anyone, "What is racism?" and they'll likely answer that it is white bias against people of color, that it is oppression rooted in racial and/or ethnic group membership.

They are not wrong in describing what racism looks like *externally*.

Often overlooked is *internalized* racism, something subtler and more insidious. When racism is the cultural norm, Black and Indigenous people of color (BIPOC) raised in such a society can internalize harmful racial narratives, subconsciously and even consciously. We may unintentionally reinforce ideas about ourselves and the world that collude with racism, leading to self-doubt, self-loathing, and self-disrespect. Racism perpetuates itself on a deep, inner, and subconscious level that traumatizes us and undermines our true power. For the BIPOC community, this book provides a path toward personal healing.

Internalized racism in white people can also be subconsciously insidious. Generations of white dominance and political power has led many of them to rarely, if ever, think about their privilege blindness and how their deeply rooted preconceptions precipitate microaggressions. They may tokenize others, assume criminality, expect lower intellectual capacity, claim colorblindness, or disrespect different communication styles. Internalized racism in white people can prompt an inner voice that says, "But I'm not racist—that's *other* people." This sustains the lack of responsibility that perpetuates a structurally racist society. Yes, "good people" and "bad people" can be racist. For white readers, this book provides actions to break that cycle and answers the ever-present question, "What can I do?"

Tarot for the Hard Work is a tool for passionately demolishing structural oppression. It is a tool for white people who want to use their privilege for mass liberation. It is a tool for Black and Brown people living in a structurally racist society intent on selling self-hatred and shame to marginalized people and capitalizing on their pain. It is a tool for both tarot newbies and tarot experts. It is a tool for action. It is a tool for going beyond baby steps. It is a tool that can offer great satisfaction as well as great difficulty. It is a tool to expand your comfort zone. This is a tool that requires your presence for it to work.

I'm an unapologetically Black writer, tarot reader, ritual facilitator, and artist whose work ultimately prioritizes one thing: freedom. I'll be your guide as we explore the Major Arcana to uncover how each archetype can help us cultivate a freer world. As we move through the cards, from the Fool to the World, keep in mind that everything we do ripples beyond us and that we must take responsibility for our actions. We'll seek opportunities for liberation within ourselves, our relationships, and our communities. Bless the interconnectedness of all things, for it promises that our magic is about more than ourselves!

The fact that I'm your guide doesn't mean that I have all the answers. This book exists because of my blog series about antiracism and tarot. I discussed various manifestations of racism and everyday strategies to combat it. It felt terrifying to write about these things on the internet, a place where I've been vulnerable to racist attacks. Being invisible was safe, but some things are more important than our individual safety.

The Moon card reflects how our subconscious has a way of boiling to the surface until it can no longer be ignored. Writing the blog, two things fascinated me:

1. People actually use the strategies I've written about in the real world!

2. Wow, I have a *lot* of internalized racism to unpack.

As I said, I don't have all the answers. I'm right there with you, experimenting with creative ways to use my spiritual practice toward a more liberated planet upon the smoldering ashes of white supremacy. I chose to write about antiracism strategies using the Major Arcana because of the powerful impact that tarot has had on me. Tarot helped me heal past trauma, communicate with the spirit realm, process two near-death experiences, and so much more. I know how this resource has affected my life, as well as my darling clients' lives. With tarot, we embody unique archetypes to energize different parts of ourselves to deepen our lives. If we can use tarot to inspire and enlighten personal evolution, why can't we do the same with community transformation?

Our focus will remain mostly on the tarot, but please incorporate any other ethical tools, spiritual or otherwise, into your antiracism work. Each chapter will focus on one Major Arcana card and will feature

- Multiple perspectives of each Major Arcana card and how they show up in internalized and societal racism

- How the shadow shows up in each card and different ways to use the benevolent aspects of each card to confront it

- Activities to dismantle internalized racism, interpersonal racism, and racism in communities

- Thoughtful reflection prompts

- Inspirational mantras

I would like to draw your attention to bullet point #3: **Activities**. This book is about action: taking action, changing action, becoming aware of action. Each chapter is going to present activities that will ask you to reflect on how you manifest and act upon the energy of each card. There will be questions. There will be exercises. There will be places where you'll want and need to record your thoughts and impressions. I highly encourage you to buy a journal (or two!) so that you can participate in these activities as we go along. Look for this prompt for journaling exercises and activities: ✎

Of course, I could have asked you to fill in a blank on the page, but the number of activities in this book would have made it an unwieldy tome. And more importantly, I don't want to presume your thoughts and exercise entries would even fit onto one or two lines. A journal will give you unlimited space to explore and do a dive deep: *in your journal you are writing your own antiracism manifesto.*

Your experience through this book should not feel fixed, prescriptive, or dogmatic. Tarot is a flexible analog for our life experiences. If our lives and world are always changing, then so should our tarot practice and freedom work. I want you to interact with the tarot archetypes more intuitively. In our instant gratification information-age world, it can be tempting to take someone's perspective and run with it. Instead, take what resonates with you and forget the rest. I want this work to feel *personal*. I want you to strengthen your personal relationship with the cards. One reason I'm a tarot reader is the reality that tarot is most effective when intuitively guided and manifested consciously. As you incorporate new information and activities in your everyday life, try to

- Take ownership over your actions and their consequences
- Use whatever privilege you have responsibly and often
- Remain open, aware, and flexible
- Reflect regularly
- Confess, apologize, and fix your mistakes
- Listen
- Act!

This work isn't supposed to be easy. One could imagine where we'd be if it was. Our commitment to a radically evolved future means committing *now* to radical action and change. You might find that even minor changes can feel uncomfortable. Right now is a good time to accept that fact, anticipate some bumpy roads, and start where you are. We must get through the Tower to make it to the Star.

If you're reading this book, you probably already have a few things in your "witch toolbox." Maybe you have gems, candles, meditations, or whatnot. Lean on the magic that ignites your path to awareness, insight, and social change. There is one hard rule, though: you must understand that you are the most magical ingredient of your life. No rune or naked dance in the woods could hold a flame to your inherent magic. You may have companions, but ultimately you are the one who moves your energy. This book is a spell for our more ideal futures, forged by intention, willpower, action, and compassion.

In my Jewish tradition, we often speak of "the world to come," the future we are constantly building with spirit guidance, community responsibility, and acts of devotion. I talked about this a few times with Rabbi Mychal Copeland of the Sha'ar Zahav synagogue in San Francisco. She once told me that some people recast the phrase as "the world that is coming." I like that one better.

I believe in a better future. I believe in it because we are already building it.

One last thing: I'm only one person. I write this book from a perspective of a Black woman raised in the United States. I can't divorce that fact from anything I do in the public sphere. Still, the strategies and exercises in this book can help you confront racism of all kinds.

The future is on its way. Let's go, witches.

0

THE FOOL

We are the ones we've been waiting for.

—JUNE JORDAN

Inhaling and exhaling deeply, the Fool awkwardly yet boldly appears: a trouble-maker, a risk-taker, someone who doesn't—and knows they don't—have the answers. Some people see the Fool as a blank slate, the epitome of pure, unfiltered potential. But being human means that we show up to all new experiences with baggage like preconceptions, memories, and biases. This realization fuels the Fool's journey. All experiences are tinted by the person experiencing them. One's story is one's perception of an experience. As such, one must look before they leap.

Just as they're not afraid to enter unfamiliar spaces, the Fool isn't afraid to disrupt the status quo. Simply their presence in oppressive spaces is a statement punctuated by their will to do the work. For a spell to work, it requires intention, will, and action. The Fool envisions a more ideal future and intends to make it so. They move through new structures, doggedly committed to acting upon their intention even when it scares them. Then they leap without clear knowledge of exactly where they'll land. They just know that something in themselves or their world needs to change.

They're here to make what civil rights activist John Lewis called "good trouble."

The Fool jumps into the unknown as a child, hungry for new experiences and ready to learn. This is the beginning of all the creativity that they will use in their approach to social justice. The Fool explores unfamiliar, liminal spaces with even just the slightest confidence that they are divinely protected.

The Fool can

- Have a strong appetite for life
- Move with a sense of freedom
- Have an unchained spirit
- Show up through unconventional paths
- Be a dreamer
- Show immense passion about their ideas

Embodied Keywords

Pull out the Fool card from one deck or several. Take a deep breath and pause. Gaze at the imagery. From a liberation perspective, envision yourself in the card's landscape. Be the archetype. Name some keywords that you personally associate with this card. Remember, your definitions are more relevant to your tarot reading than what's in the little white book. Here are a few keywords to help get you started.

> Potential, new beginnings, fresh starts, spontaneity, inspiration, readiness to taste for the first time, optimism, courage, taking risks, protection

✎ **Your keywords:** _____

The Fool in Liberation Work

The Fool approaches liberation work with tenacious curiosity and determination. They're new to this path, but they know and accept that it will be uncomfortable and difficult. They're inspired to make a move, but they must beware burnout. Antiracism work is long game work. Going full force and burning out don't serve the collective as much as consistent devotion and frequent rest.

The Fool is quite inquisitive. After all, they're pursuing a world that no one has ever before seen: They must be wide-eyed, especially if they're looking before they leap. They learn from more experienced people about existing theory and practice, recognizing that there's room for their unique contributions. Whether the Fool takes their antiracism work to their office or to their parents, they mindfully curate their efforts to their abilities and their environments. The Fool expects adaptation. They're prepared to mold themselves and shift form when they learn new information and whenever the moment requires.

In decks inspired by the Rider-Waite-Smith Tarot, the Fool often carries a tiny knapsack in which they store inspiration to fuel their work. They might treat it as a fertile altar, something to water, sing to, ground, protect, confess to, plan with, meditate upon, channel ancestors (living or passed on, blood-related or not) with, and generously care for. This altar becomes a traveling home for the Fool, a source of familiarity and renewal when they feel like quitting. They anticipate the temptation to resign and prepare for those almost-inevitable bumps in the spiral roads of societal evolution.

The Fool is ready to be a stranger in a strange land, where they'll need to learn from their mistakes and listen to others' narratives of oppression. This archetype commits to honoring and respecting victims' stories. There is a constant that runs through the Fool's mind reminding them to be consistently honest about their prejudices and influences in order to heal from their oppressive beliefs and habits. They might squirm, but they're going to confront their internalized racism, no matter their race.

The Fool is ready to do the work, and they set off to do it with energetic sustainability.

Correspondences for Inspiration

Consider exploring sources of inspiration that you associate with the Fool. To help get you started, here are a few popular correspondences.

> Insects (particularly butterflies), birds, crocodiles, the air element, bamboo, almond, pine, papyrus, lavender, ferns, peppermint, one's chest, the scent of grass, clear quartz, chalcedony, tin, topaz, evergreen trees

✎ What reminds you of the Fool? How do these things inspire you to keep going?

How the Fool Can Show Up

There are as many interpretations of tarot as there are people who have ever lived. There is no completely universal card interpretation because there is no completely universal perspective on life. Your and your clients' interpretations are what matter the most during a reading. Of all the possible magical ingredients, we humans are the most powerful in enacting real-world change. However, there are strong collective energies around the themes that appear more frequently when a particular archetype shows up. Here are some of those common motifs.

THE BALANCED FOOL

- Ready to get uncomfortable
- Willing to learn
- Open to change
- Courageous
- Asks for help
- Craves a challenge

✎ My relationship to the Fool feels balanced when _____

THE IMBALANCED FOOL

- Naïve
- Held back by fear of judgment
- Doubtful
- Deliberately ignorant
- Reckless
- Fixed on what an activist "should" look like

✎ My relationship to the Fool feels imbalanced when _____

Leaping into Radical Discomfort

A note about structure: The first three cards, the Fool, Magician, and High Priestess, center on preparation. Afterward we'll dive into specific topics and additional exercises, starting with the Empress. Even though this book has a beginning and an end, you will benefit from envisioning the Major Arcana as a circle rather than a line, where the end is also the beginning. Or better yet, as a thing with no prescribed order but the one that makes sense for any given intention.

The Void welcomes you.

The Fool lives at the beginning, at the end, and wherever we need them in between. At this juncture, you're ready to leap into the Void, where all possibility incubates—even if it feels like a risk, a shot in the dark.

But look before you move past go! Take stock of your privilege and the ways that you perpetuate structural racism in your everyday life. Get so honest with yourself that it hurts. Then go deeper. Notice where your attention flows. Notice when you squirm. Notice when and how you resist. It is a tender confrontation to realize how your everyday actions indisputably connect to the oppression, torture, and murder of Black and Brown people around the world. You might not know anyone who lives in Cancer Alley, but I bet you've purchased plenty of things made of synthetic rubber without considering their origin. And maybe you've never had a relative or friend murdered by the police, but I'm sure you remember Trayvon, Sandra, George, among so many others.

We can't know everything (including how the global majority experience life on a largely anti-BIPOC planet), but change often requires hurtling into the unknown, vaulting into learning and unlearning—listening, absorbing, acting, reflecting. The risk of learning is that we can uncover things that are painful, difficult, or, at the very least, inconvenient. Yet the risk of our ignorance is far greater than the risk of shame.

This is the point where you accept that change often requires great discomfort. This work is not supposed to be easy. It's not supposed to be comfortable. Especially for white people, dismantling racism is supposed to be arduous, specifically because it requires you to lose power in order to redistribute it.

So jump into the void and submit to discomfort. Risk-taking is transcendent work. Ending structural racism is not a linear journey. It is an iterative process that wears many faces and takes many avenues. Maybe you don't know what the work is yet, but paying attention is a start. Or maybe you've done plenty of work. Now is the time to dive deeper. Possibility matters, but only when we lean into it.

Identifying as the Fool

How do you already embody the Fool? Use this list of words commonly associated with this card to identify the qualities that you do and don't want to work with as you help create a radically more equitable world.

- Circle the qualities you already embody and can leverage as a superpower.
- Draw a heart around the qualities you want to embody more deeply or frequently.
- Draw a square around the qualities you want to transmute or avoid.

Bold	Curious	Rigid	Flexible
Spontaneous	Insecure	Intentional	Creative
Reckless	Has unclear motivations	Has specific expectations	Scared
Easily distracted	Adventurous	Careless	Aware
Has student mindset	Reluctant	Prepared	Humble

Affirmations for Embodying the Fool

As you step into the mysterious realm of the Fool, you might choose an affirmation to motivate you when the work is difficult. Affirmations can strengthen commitment by supporting your confidence in achieving personal and community goals. They can also help combat fear, anxiety, self-doubt, and loss of motivation, which are common feelings that come up in social justice work. You can chant them, write them down, meditate on them, add them to your phone background, or otherwise work with them consistently to keep focused on your objectives. Here are some examples.

"Every day, I commit to the work in a new way."

"In this body, in this moment, in this place, I am ready."

"I believe in a future I cannot see."

"My life is intentional."

"I am protected everywhere I go."

Often, the most powerful affirmations are the ones we create for ourselves. Take some time to jot down your personal affirmations.

Magical Practices to Conjure the Fool

Create an inspiration file or board. Practice taking small risks every day. Envision your potential. Talk to other people who are doing the work. Practice grounding. Work with Uranus. Make a new moon intention. Become more curious. Do research. Examine your motivations. Explore different approaches. Learn about the people around you and in your community. Start analyzing everyday actions and structures. Name your privileges. Hone your natural skills. Notice, notice, notice.

Becoming the Fool

Meditate on your relationship with the Fool and use your observations to plan real-world action. By responding to these prompts, you are committing to doing the work—period.

SET A PERSONAL, RELATIONAL, OR COLLECTIVE INTENTION

 Name an objective that your work will center around.

 Plan specific actions for this objective that you will take as you embody the Fool.

 This [day/week/month/event], I will embody the Fool in my liberation work by

_____

 This work is important because _____

 The affirmation I will repeat is _____

REFLECT ON YOUR EXPERIENCE

 Evolution is iterative and often nonlinear. As we pursue our goals, we must regularly evaluate our actions, mistakes, and learnings to inform the next cycles of change. Review your experience and identify what you can take with you as you move through your antiracism work.

- Successes

- Setbacks

- Frustrations

- Questions

- Other reflections

- Next steps

BUILDING A TOOLKIT

Write Your Racial Healing Glossary

As the Fool, you courageously plunge into an undefined, amorphous space. Familiarize yourself with the road signs on your expedition by thoughtfully researching and describing what common antiracism terms mean for your work.

Accomplice _____

Ally _____

Coconspirator _____

Cultural appreciation _____

Cultural appropriation _____

Equality _____

Equity _____

Generalization _____

Implicit bias _____

Internalized racism _____

Intersectionality_____

Power _____

Prejudice _____

Privilege_____

Racism _____

Reverse racism _____

Stereotype_____

Systematic_____

Systemic _____

White supremacy_____

White supremacy culture _____

1

THE MAGICIAN

A man who stands for nothing will fall for anything.

—MALCOLM X

As the witches say, "As above, so below." The Magician is a channel between dreams and reality. They say yes to their personal magic and generously offer the world their existing knowledge, experience, and skills. Possibility and desire precipitate the Magician's will to use and expand this unique tool set.

The Magician is a strategist who is (or wants to be) skilled in planning tangible action. At this point in their journey, they haven't collected many new tools. They must rely on what's already in their knapsack. Thus, they must be inventive. They must be bold. Only untraditional actions can shift communities away from traditional harm.

The Magician, often associated with the planet Mercury, represents the number one in the Major Arcana. As one is associated with Mars, the Magician has a bubbling, restless desire to enact change. Mercury reveals the Magician as a card of the mind, of visions and concentration. When Mercury's visions and focus combine with Mars's will to act, the Magician becomes a bridge between mental and physical worlds. They devote themselves to creating the world they want to inhabit.

This archetype knows when to clean their energetic house. They analyze how they spend their attention to identify distractions to circumvent, integrate, or remove. Simone Weil wrote, "Attention is the rarest and purest form of generosity." The Magician is generous in their anti-oppression work when they continually focus their lens on personal and community antiracism goals.

The Magician never forgets the difference between "power over" and "power with." Meditate upon the difference.

The Magician can

- Be a dynamic mover and shaker
- Invent creative and resourceful solutions to tangible problems
- Confront challenges head-on
- Set goals and plan action effectively
- Know when goals are attainable
- Serve as a city planner, project manager, mechanic, or alchemist

Embodied Keywords

Pull out the Magician card from one deck or several. Take a deep breath and pause. Gaze at the imagery. From a liberation perspective, envision yourself in the card's landscape. Be the archetype. Name some keywords that you personally associate with this card. Remember, your definitions are more relevant to your tarot reading than what's in the little white book. Here are a few keywords to help get you started.

> Concentration, beginning, engagement, power, desire, manifestation, willpower, opportunity, alchemy, conduit, skill, logic, mental clarity, fortitude

✎ Your keywords: _____

The Magician in Liberation Work

The Magician, the trailblazer, starts with what they already know. They begin their work in familiar spaces, such as work or school, identifying where they can effect change. They're wide-eyed, aware of their surroundings and how they fit into them. With their environment as a backdrop, they observe their privileges within a space and begin to leverage them for true justice.

The Magician takes advantage of their existing skills, experimentally learning how to use them in novel and practical ways. They're confident that their abilities can help change society, and they approach potential opportunities with gusto. An artist holds a fundraiser to raise money for an underserved school district. A mechanic offers sliding scale vocational classes to help people raise their financial power. A caregiver reads culturally diverse books with their children. The Magician might not know everything, but they know that they are already prepared, the best they can, to begin new initiatives. They represent magic unto itself.

This archetype always keeps their motivations on their radar. They expect that competing messages and conflicting needs will influence their evolving mindset. Whenever the Magician recognizes that their actions are selfish or misguided, they promptly correct course. For instance, if they learn that their nonprofit employer has a history of silencing marginalized voices, they use intent and determination to act upon that information.

The Magician does work that energizes them. They are more effective when they're in their element, so they won't take actions simply because "that's what activists are supposed to do." They know that it takes many kinds of people to change the world and that they are the only person who can deliver through their specific style of magic.

Correspondences for Inspiration

Consider exploring sources of inspiration that you connect with the Magician. To help get you started, here are a few popular associations.

> Coyotes, foxes, nightingales, ibises, vervain, clover, lily of the valley, wildflowers, roses, fennel, marjoram, citrus peels, odiferous seeds, agate, opal, emerald, mixed metals, ouroboros symbol

✎ What reminds you of the Magician? How do these things inspire you to keep going?

How the Magician Can Show Up

There are as many interpretations of tarot as there are people who have ever lived. There is no completely universal card interpretation because there is no completely universal perspective on life. Your and your clients' interpretations are what matter the most during a reading. Of all the possible magical ingredients, we humans are the most powerful in enacting real-world change. However, there are strong collective energies around the themes that appear more frequently when a particular archetype shows up. Here are some of those common motifs.

THE BALANCED MAGICIAN

- Innovative
- Willing to try different approaches
- Energetic and motivated
- Focused
- Resourceful
- Experimental

My relationship to the Magician feels balanced when _____

THE IMBALANCED MAGICIAN

- Always does things "by the book"
- Misuses knowledge and power
- Desires personal gain
- Tricks and manipulates
- Needs grounding
- Underutilizes key talents

My relationship to the Magician feels imbalanced when _____

Becoming a Vessel

A note about structure: The first three cards, the Fool, Magician, and High Priestess, center on preparation. Afterward we'll dive into specific topics and additional exercises, starting with the Empress. Even though this book has a beginning and an end, you will benefit from envisioning the Major Arcana as a circle rather than a line, where the end is also the beginning. Or better yet, as a thing with no prescribed order but the one that makes sense for any given intention.

You are a vessel.

You are magic, and your magic can work through your will. Will is the result of possibility, desire, and action. To harness your will to effect real-world change, you must believe in the possibility of change and hold a clear desire.

The Magician calls you to examine your intention behind antiracism work and whether you truly believe in your intention. It may feel like the goalpost is too far into the distance to be realistic. Do you genuinely believe that a world without structural oppression is possible?

It's okay to say no, given historical and current contexts. However, it is not okay to stay there.

The Magician creates magic because they believe real change is possible. Your intention will never be as powerful as it needs to be if you don't believe that structural racism's death is possible. Whatever else could be your intention? How could you ever truly prioritize this immediate and critical work over the natural desire for convenience if you genuinely did not believe, in the deepest home of your heart, that social change is absolutely realizable?

It is possible to dream in tangible reality.

What is it that you desire at the end of this work? Be both broad and specific. The work becomes meaningful in our mundane lives—our interactions, perceptions, experiences, and choices—when there is an authentic motivation behind it.

But don't be so fixed on your motivation that you prevent yourself from continual learning and listening!

Can you visualize a completely equitable society? Many unconsciously deprioritize this work because they don't genuinely think it is achievable. They choose not to dream beyond what they have seen. The work becomes less about the dismantlement of the oppressive state and more about keeping the peace. Passive racism is what keeps structural racism alive You must trust that change is conceivable or this work will never be as important to you as the world needs it to be.

When you step into this spell, expect no pats on the back. Expect discomfort, ridicule, and the regular loss of the things that your privilege has afforded you. Expect your level of convenience to change, as well as your relationships, finances, material possessions, media consumption, and more. Your intention is an anchor you can hold on to when you're experiencing discomfort or disappointment. If you expect this work to be easy, return to the lessons of the Fool.

So why are you here, and why will you be here every single day?

SUGGESTED EXERCISES

1. Identify and articulate your intention. Keep a representation of your intention in a place where you'll notice it every day. For example, you may write a note on a bookmark, put a Post-it on your bathroom mirror, or tape a photo of someone who inspires your mission onto a water bottle.

2. Establish a practice of consuming new media, ideally minority-led, on a weekly basis that helps you remain both focused on and aware of the different, evolving ways you can act intentionally.

3. Create a daily habit of integrating your intention into your spiritual practice. Use a more inclusive tarot deck, invite and include BIPOC in your circles, harness the spell of wealth redistribution by how you structure your offerings, or establish another routine that integrates the work of antiracism into your spirituality. Reflect upon how these decisions parallel other decisions you can make in your everyday life beyond the altar.

Identifying as the Magician

How do you already embody the Magician? Use this list of words commonly associated with this card to identify the qualities that you do and don't want to work with as you help create a radically more equitable world.

- Circle the qualities you already embody and can leverage as a superpower.

- Draw a heart around the qualities you want to embody more deeply or frequently.

- Draw a square around the qualities you want to transmute or avoid.

Alchemist	Willing to engage	Intentional	Willing to adjust	Grounded
Powerful	Shy about abilities	Acts performatively	Self-aware	Resourceful
Insecure	Good at puzzles	Empowered	Ego-driven	Motivated
Impatience	Able to concentrate	Easily distracted	Desires to create	Confrontational

Affirmations for Embodying the Magician

As you step into the industrious realm of the Magician, you might choose an affirmation to motivate you when the work is difficult. Affirmations can strengthen commitment by supporting your confidence in achieving personal and community goals. They can also help combat fear, anxiety, self-doubt, and loss of motivation, which are common feelings that come up in social justice work. You can chant them, write them down, meditate on them, add them to your phone background, or otherwise work with them consistently to keep focused on your objectives. Here are some examples.

"The world needs my magic."

"I am the only one who can do what I do the way I do it."

"I make things real."

"I am actively building the world to come."

"I am divinely empowered to begin."

✎ Often, the most powerful affirmations are the ones we create for ourselves. Take some time to jot down your personal affirmations.

Magical Practices to Conjure the Magician

List skills and knowledge you want to use. Learn from experienced activists. Say yes. Begin a creative practice. Define what commitment looks like for you. Work with Mercury and Mars. Accept and integrate feedback. Meditate more often. Ground yourself daily. List ways you can use your privilege for good. Identify social structures you will disrupt. Become a skilled volunteer. Know your ultimate intention.

Becoming the Magician

Meditate on your relationship with the Magician and use what you know to plan real-world action. By responding to these prompts, you are committing to doing the work—period.

SET A PERSONAL, RELATIONAL, OR COLLECTIVE INTENTION

✎ Name an objective that your work will center around.

✎ Plan specific actions for this objective that you will take as you embody the Magician.

✎ This [day/week/month/event], I will embody the Magician in my liberation work by _____

✎ This work is important because _____

✎ The affirmation I will repeat is _____

REFLECT ON YOUR EXPERIENCE

✎ Evolution is iterative and often nonlinear. As we pursue our goals, we must regularly evaluate our actions, mistakes, and learnings to inform the next cycles of change. Review your experience and identify what you can take with you as you move through your antiracism work.

- Successes

- Setbacks

- Frustrations

- Questions

- Other reflections

- Next steps

BUILDING A TOOLKIT

Ground Your Whys and Hows

WHY AM I DOING THIS?

Embodying the Magician means naming and believing in your intentions for a better world. To do this, your intentions must be clear and actionable. Clarify your intentions with these reflective prompts.

What lived experiences push me to do antiracism work now?

When have I witnessed racism?

How do I currently perpetuate racism?

What are my nonliving ancestors' experiences with racism?

What are my family's experiences with racism?

What are my friends' experiences with racism?

How does racism show up in my community spaces, such as witch covens or city parks?

What are some outdated racist beliefs I once held? How have these beliefs changed?

When have I ignored opportunities to act upon racial justice? What would I instead do now?

HOW AM I DOING THIS?

Showing up as the Magician means knowing one's skills and being willing to begin where they are. Use this space to list skills you can use, hone, and teach others.

Skills I Will Use _____

Skills I Will Improve_____

Skills I Can Teach Others_____ _____

2

THE HIGH PRIESTESS

Look for me in the whirlwind or the storm.
—MARCUS GARVEY

The Magician leverages magic. The High Priestess *is* magic.

In spiral time, the High Priestess thoughtfully creeps into the dark. They don't move just for themselves—they've got the collective on their mind. Beyond the Magician's ego, the High Priestess wields a wider lens that more intentionally includes the greater collective. Intuitively guided, the High Priestess enters liminal spaces, boldly confronting internal and external shadows to glean information for the world they actively live in. They always return from the unknown.

As the High Priestess cycles back to the known, their new insights inspire their actions and others'. They disseminate knowledge through language, action, and energy, all in the name of collective healing.

This empathetic archetype confronts their flaws and ways they perpetuate harm. The High Priestess realizes that this work is often heavy and can conjure shame. The work can feel more overwhelming knowing how much internal and external work there is to be done. Wide-eyed and strong willed, they still peer into the truth because noticing is the first step in illuminating possibilities of change. To notice more deliberately, the High Priestess exercises their intuition frequently.

In this card, one can channel glimpses of the celestial relationship between the Moon and Vulcan. Vulcan tends the fire that keeps the High Priestess's intention warm as they explore the shadows with lunar sensitivity and depth. This archetype needs to maintain clear motivation while remaining open to the mysteries in the deep.

The High Priestess can

- Know intuitively where to focus their attention
- Be willing to get uncomfortable
- Have great detective skills
- Exhibit independence and self-sufficiency
- Not only dream, but sincerely believe in their dreams
- Serve as a consultant, coach, therapist, or advisor

Embodied Keywords

Pull out the High Priestess card from one deck or several. Take a deep breath and pause. Gaze at the imagery. From a liberation perspective, envision yourself in the card's landscape. Be the archetype. Name some keywords that you personally associate with this card. Remember, your definitions are more relevant to your tarot reading than what's in the little white book. Here are a few keywords to help get you started.

> Intuition, receptivity, permission to embody magic, symbology, mystery, subconscious, wisdom, water, initial encounters with the "other," dream messages, universal knowledge, spirit guides, empathy

✎ **Your keywords:** _____

The High Priestess in Liberation Work

The High Priestess is a visionary, receiving and translating intuitive downloads to help guide people in liberation work. They are a channel between the seen and the unseen, courageous enough to confront the parts of themselves and their communities that are ugly, repressed, and purposely ignored. Their power may be quiet, some may say passive. But make no mistake, the High Priestess is undoubtedly an active participant in their world. They might just need some space and quiet to figure out how to communicate their new knowledge in effective, action-oriented, and inspiring ways.

The High Priestess doesn't believe that they have a "higher self." They are who they are, no matter where they are within and between the worlds. Sometimes they show up as their idea of an activist, other times they're just grateful that they put on pants on a Sunday. The High Priestess is many things at once, while contained in a complete sense of self. They are aware of their personal complexities and how new information can complicate internal and external relationships. The work isn't linear, so there's space to put things on the table. The work is complicated because we are complicated, because our world is complicated.

The High Priestess doesn't just visit different environments, they experience them. They show up to neighborhoods they've never been, confront strangers, and witness evidence they know they'll never forget. The High Priestess is the witness, not the hero. They're the oracle, not the prophecy. They gaze into overlooked cracks and crevices to see the ignominious truths about the white supremacist culture they live in and are a part of—no matter what race. They listen to and learn from marginalized people. They don't demand emotional labor; they just observe the rawness. As they act upon what they learn, they scale their efforts by disseminating those stories and lessons so that their impact is greater than what they keep to themselves. The High Priestess is not a gatekeeper.

That which illuminates the truth illuminates the High Priestess's path toward a healed future.

Correspondences for Inspiration

Consider exploring sources of inspiration that you associate with the High Priestess. To help get you started, here are a few popular ones.

Dung beetles, deer, camels, cats, bears, hyssop, olives, pomegranate, lily, lotus, jasmine, mushrooms, poppy, potato, melons, cabbage, egg whites, sweet odors, moonstone, pearl, selenite, aquamarine, lapis lazuli, kyanite

✎ **What reminds you of the High Priestess? How do these things inspire you to keep going?**

How the High Priestess Can Show Up

There are as many interpretations of tarot as there are people who have ever lived. There is no completely universal card interpretation because there is no completely universal perspective on life. Your and your clients' interpretations are what matter the most during a reading. Of all the possible magical ingredients, we humans are the most powerful in enacting real-world change. However, there are strong collective energies around the themes that appear more frequently when a particular archetype shows up. Here are some of those common motifs.

THE BALANCED HIGH PRIESTESS

- Innovative
- Willing to try different approaches
- Energetic and motivated
- Focused
- Resourceful
- Experimental
- Attuned to intuition

✎ My relationship to the High Priestess feels balanced when _____

THE IMBALANCED HIGH PRIESTESS

- Hoards information
- Misuses knowledge and power
- Desires personal gain
- Tricks and manipulates
- Needs grounding
- Underutilizes key talents
- Ignores intuition

✎ My relationship to the High Priestess feels imbalanced when _____

Reenvisioning Love and Light

A note about structure: The first three cards, the Fool, Magician, and High Priestess, center on preparation. Afterward we'll dive into specific topics and additional exercises, starting with the Empress. Even though this book has a beginning and an end, you will benefit from envisioning the Major Arcana as a circle rather than a line, where the end is also the beginning. Or better yet, as a thing with no prescribed order but the one that makes sense for any given intention.

After gazing into yourself, gaze into the other.

Quite often, the "love and light" perspective conceals devastating truths behind the oppression that enables spiritual bypassing practices and rhetoric. It's a veil, asserting total serenity in a world where peace is often a foreign concept. One of a witch's duties is to effect real change in the real world. And the real world is not all love and light.

The High Priestess instructs us to go beyond the veil, to overcome our discomfort and our fears to gaze at our shadows. These things might feel unfamiliar, but they have been there all along. Then they encourage us to take what we've discovered in the dark and bring it into the light so we can transform that information into a thing that serves something bigger than ourselves. Our knowledge is useless until it is used. Confronting your internalized racism and your oppressive actions is a commitment to the world.

We take so much from the world. We must reciprocate.

Analyze your inner voice. Can you always trust it when it has inevitably been influenced by your participatory existence in a racist society with complex capitalistic roots are enforced by de facto subjugation? The love and light crowd tells us to always trust our inner voices. Yet how can we say everyone should always trust their feelings when people, with the deepest convictions, use their feelings to justify everything from microaggressions to gatekeeping to murder?

The work of trusting our feelings involves the continual, never-ending work of cultivating **active** empathy. It also includes the healthy pressure of knowing that this empathy can atrophy whenever we autopilot our habits, perspectives, sources of inspiration, and permissions.

Yes, so many of us are overworked, overpressured, and overstimulated, and we all set to autopilot sometimes. Still, aim to be as intentional as possible about how you use your inner knowledge in the world.

Consider how the pursuit of equity requires that the oppressor constantly loses something—comfort, money, connections, time, etc.—or else their work is passive, virtuous by label rather than action.

So what can you do to deepen and activate your empathy so that your feelings become not facts, but rather increasingly trustworthy compasses to help guide your everyday choices?

Consider where your money goes.

Consider the people around you.

Consider the events you attend.

Consider your spiritual practices and tools.

Consider where you get your information from.

Consider where your sources got their sources.

Consider the excuses you make.

Consider the stories you hear.

Consider the stories you tell yourself.

Consider getting uncomfortable.

Go into dark places. Learn, absorb, integrate. Continually decentralize the racism in your inner voice. Facing and working on your own darkness are acts of genuine love and light to the world.

SUGGESTED EXERCISES

1. Watch "Reframing Internalized Racial Oppression: Shifting Our Theory of Oppression" by Dr. Kira Hudson Banks.

2. Take Project Implicit's How We Think About Race/Ethnicity test, even if you've done it before; then reflect on your results.

3. Explore and subscribe to nonwhite media sources.

4. Read *Why Are All the Black Kids Sitting Together in the Cafeteria? And Other Conversations About Race* by Beverly Daniel Tatum.

Identifying as the High Priestess

How do you already embody the High Priestess? Use this list of words commonly associated with this card to identify the qualities that you do and don't want to work with as you help create a radically more equitable world.

- Circle the qualities you already embody and can leverage as a superpower.

- Draw a heart around the qualities you want to embody more deeply or frequently.

- Draw a square around the qualities you want to transmute or avoid.

Introspective	Curious	Selfish	Humble
Superficial	Wise	Skeptical	Has secret agendas
Guardian	Dualistic	Hoards information	Uses knowledge to dominate
Frantic	Defensive	Patient	Acts swiftly	Doubts their magic
Empathetic	Lives in echo chambers	Comfortable with unknowns	

Affirmations for Embodying the High Priestess

As you step into the liminal realm of the High Priestess, you might choose an affirmation to motivate you when the work is difficult. Affirmations can strengthen commitment by supporting your confidence in achieving personal and community goals. They can also help combat fear, anxiety, self-doubt, and loss of motivation, which are common feelings that come up in social justice work. You can chant them, write them down, meditate on them, add them to your phone background, or otherwise work with them consistently to keep focused on your objectives. Here are some examples.

"I am the vessel and I am the catalyst."

"Nothing I learn is only for me."

"I evolve in many timelines."

"I can learn something anywhere I go."

"My internal work shapes my external world."

✎ Often, the most powerful affirmations are the ones we create for ourselves. Take some time to jot down your personal affirmations.

Magical Practices to Conjure the High Priestess

Speak up in spaces dominated by white feminism. Eat pomegranates. Defend trans women. Become a lifelong learner. Go to therapy. Evolve what you share online. Try lunar living. Accept that you will never know everything. Illuminate the stories and initiatives of people with less privilege or visibility than you. Practice noticing through stream-of-consciousness journaling. Read things that make you uncomfortable. Audit your spiritual habits for oppressive practices. Show up to action planning meetings you've never attended. Get out of your comfort zone.

Becoming the High Priestess

Meditate on your relationship with the High Priestess, and use what you know to plan real-world action. By responding to these prompts, you are committing to doing the work—period.

SET A PERSONAL, RELATIONAL, OR COLLECTIVE INTENTION

✎ Name an objective that your work will center around.

✎ Plan specific actions for this objective that you will take as you embody the High Priestess.

✎ This [day/week/month/event], I will embody the High Priestess in my liberation work by _____

✎ This work is important because _____

✎ The affirmation I will repeat is _____

REFLECT ON YOUR EXPERIENCE

✎ Evolution is iterative and often nonlinear. As we pursue our goals, we must regularly evaluate our actions, mistakes, and learnings to inform the next cycles of change. Review your experience and identify what you can take with you as you move through your antiracism work.

- Successes

- Setbacks

- Frustrations

- Questions

- Other reflections

- Next steps

Set Your Intentions

The High Priestess lives within and between worlds. They're here and there, in shadows and in light, internal and external, swimming in water and wheeling on land. We, too, live within and between worlds. Our physical bodies may inhabit only one space at a time, but our actions always ripple outward and leave traces in places we may never guess. The High Priestess reminds us to watch our surroundings for connections. Despite the purposely oppressive design of modern cities, the reality is that our lives are never truly isolated.

People can enter antiracism work with a bevy of goals. These goals may be amorphous and without clear vision, which is natural. The basic idea is that we all just want the world to "be better." Yet pausing to clarify our goals offers us a guiding hand as we enter mysterious futures. Tomorrow is unknown, but your vision gets you there when it drives the actions you take today.

Name the three primary goals you want to reach within one year:

Goal for myself: _____

Goal for my relationships: _____

Goal for my community: _____

Then describe how all three goals relate to each other. How do they support or contradict one another? Can you plan actions that include multiple goals? What do your goals say about your confidence in your ability to step up?

3

THE EMPRESS

We can say "Peace on Earth." We can sing about it, preach about it, or pray about it, but if we have not internalized the mythology to make it happen inside us, then it will not be.

—BETTY SHABAZZ

All liberation work is creative work because our job is to create the world to come. And in waltzes the Empress.

One point is a point. Two points make a line. And three lines together make a triangle: the first form, a structure, a stool, something real. Representing key three, the Empress is both the creator and the creation as they cultivate more equitable futures through rhythm, care, and persistence. They are a generator, a textured force integrating qualities of the previous three cards: the Fool's intentional start, the Magician's power, and the High Priestess's surrender to the unknown. As such, the Empress is a gardener who starts with a seed, sows with tools, and holds faith that their plant will sprout as intended—or better than planned, as witches often make space for even more abundance in case the universe wills it to be.

Love is the Empress's guide. They know that love doesn't always look like ease or politeness. Sometimes love can look like rage and destruction when the oppressor doesn't give up without a fight. To them, love is a persistent commitment to grow and nurture their cause. They are protectors, but they're also fighters.

To perform radical acts of love, the Empress regularly tends to themselves through genuine self-care. They can't fill others' cups when theirs is bone-dry. The Empress attunes to their natural rhythms and quickly discerns when it's time to take it easy. Their work requires ingredients critical to a plant's success: space, time, and rest. They regularly reserve enough space in their lives for taking action.

They also need time; they don't expect immediate results, so they give their work time to bloom. And they prioritize rest. To constantly meddle with a plant is to deprive it of the space to grow. And so this priestess rests.

The Empress sees nature in everything: in the woods, in the garbage, in language, in bustling city crossroads. They're particularly sensitive to the interconnectedness of all things, that everything of the earth comes from the earth and returns to the earth. As such, they don't expect today's methods and strategies to work forever. New initiatives require attention, expired narratives become irrelevant in evolving discourse, and people simply change. The Empress regards how their efforts weave into the larger picture, then spring-cleans their toolshed when the seasons change.

The Empress can

- Translate data into meaningful information
- Be diligent in self-parenting
- Integrate pleasure into their work
- Have a strong abundance mentality
- Create art fearlessly
- Serve as a caregiver, mentor, gardener, or designer

Embodied Keywords

Pull out the Empress card from one deck or several. Take a deep breath and pause. Gaze at the imagery. From a liberation perspective, envision yourself in the card's landscape. Be the archetype. Name some keywords that you personally associate with this card. Remember, your definitions are more relevant to your tarot reading than what's in the little white book. Here are a few keywords to help get you started.

> Nature, fertility, creative flow, cycles, magnetism, expression, potential, community support, patience, cheerleader, form, faith, sustainability, cooperation, harmony, evolution, shared wins, seasons, generosity

 Your keywords: _____

The Empress in Liberation Work

The Empress emphasizes safety and protection in their work—not just for themselves, but also for those who don't have it. In their toolshed is a keen cognizance of their privilege. They know when to sacrifice their safety to protect others. When people feel protected enough, they're more likely to take social, physical, and financial risks—to exit their comfort zone—to fight for others' safety. The Empress truly believes that this generative cycle will continue, even if they never see all of the results. To bury a seed is to trust that it will one day break through the surface.

To the best of their ability, the empathetic Empress ensures that their comrades are nourished, literally and otherwise. They bring water and first aid to protests, start community gardens, and fundraise so that nobody goes hungry. They also care for others' emotional needs, such as by offering a listening ear, a shoulder to cry on, or a ride to a funeral.

The Empress glistens in Venus conjunct Jupiter. Venus brings cohesion to the Empress's work, and Jupiter grows that work through process. Together they prime the Empress to productively effect change. Note that Venus has seasons: the Empress's work is often cyclical, as they adjust to seasonal changes. They pay attention to the weather and act when the bellwether indicates that their garden's safety is endangered. They also notice their inner climate: they lead when they can, follow when appropriate, and rest when necessary. The Empress does not burn out.

The Empress leverages social skills for the greater good. Their Venusian influence renders them harbingers of collective gathering and attention.

Correspondences for Inspiration

Consider exploring sources of inspiration that you connect with the Empress. To help get you started, here are a few popular associations.

Bees, doves, calves, pigeons, rabbits, swans, clover, rose, hyacinth, lilac, passionflower, pear, peach, myrtle, tomatoes, saffron, flowers, patchouli, sandalwood, coriander, turquoise, brass, emerald

✎ What reminds you of the Empress? How do these things inspire you to keep going?

How the Empress Can Show Up

There are as many interpretations of tarot as there are people who have ever lived. There is no completely universal card interpretation because there is no completely universal perspective on life. Your and your clients' interpretations are what matter the most during a reading. Of all the possible magical ingredients, we humans are the most powerful in enacting real-world change. However, there are strong collective energies around the themes that appear more frequently when a particular archetype shows up. Here are some of those common motifs.

THE BALANCED EMPRESS

- Holds space
- Invests in personal evolution
- Feels secure
- Courageous enough to share their work
- Flexible
- Hands-on
- Devoted

✎ My relationship to the Empress feels balanced when _____

THE IMBALANCED EMPRESS

- Scarcity mentality
- Burns bridges
- Has difficulty cooperating
- Creatively blocked
- Exhausted
- Lacks boundaries
- Unwilling to get their hands dirty

✎ My relationship to the Empress feels imbalanced when _____

Honoring Black Womanhood

The Empress is a window into how we might use archetypical Venus and Jupiter to inform and inspire our work. Through the Empress's planetary counterpart Venus, we see the necessity of creating a world with wabi-sabi harmony, justice, and the equitable empowerment of people to not only live productive lives, but comfortable, restful, enriching, and beautiful lives. The Empress represents key three of the Major Arcana, connecting them with the inclusive, far-reaching energy of Jupiter. Our gas giant calls us to expand the work we do for humanity through intentional growth. As such, the Empress provokes us to do the work in ever-expanding ways, while keeping in mind the essential goal of creating equitable access to peace, rest, creativity, adventure, personal growth, nature, and other facets of comfortable living on Earth that are so often withheld from BIPOC.

The Empress and the topic of life's comforts often relate to the concept of the Earth mother. In *Seventy-Eight Degrees of Wisdom*, Rachel Pollack writes of the archetype, "Until we learn to experience the outer world completely, we cannot hope to transcend it." After the experience of birth with a human caregiver, a child is able to experience Mother Earth. In some spiritual beliefs, the birth correlates to the concept of the divine feminine. Yet who do we think of when we think of the divine feminine? Who gets to occupy the space of femininity that is divine?

Search "divine feminine" on Google Images and notice the trends in what you see.

Eurocentric beauty standards continually enforce a world where self-identified Black women swim through stereotypes such as the Sapphire or the mammy in order to prove that their womanhood is not even just divine, but merely valid. Meanwhile, white women are often depicted as softer and prettier, people whose womanhood must be protected at all costs. White womanhood is so tightly protected that it sometimes becomes an excuse for violence.

Enslaved Black women were not viewed as women, but as slaves. Strong, hardworking, tough. In a world where Black enslavement still exists, albeit in different forms, it's not surprising that these assumptions of Black women still exist. Unless they strive to fit into the "white ideal," then the dominant white culture categorizes them as the "something else."

Who ever said that a long-haired white woman in a flowy skirt cradling her newborn child in a field of lavender next to a tame lion is the divine feminine embodied?

Again, what do we mean by divine feminism, and who gets to occupy that space? Because I promise you:

The Black woman begging her OB-GYN to believe she's in pain—her womanhood is divine.

The Black woman CEO who has it "all together"—her womanhood is divine.

The Black woman who takes care of her grandchildren during the day, her womanhood is divine.

The Black woman with blue hair who sells her art on the corner of First and Main—her womanhood is divine.

The Black woman who scans groceries forty hours a week—her womanhood is divine.

The Black woman who persists in a world that constantly defeminizes and dehumanizes Black women—her womanhood is divine.

Yes, the Black woman is divine.

SUGGESTED EXERCISES

1. Read "As a Black Woman, I'm Tired of Having to Prove My Womanhood" by Hannah Eko.

2. Learn about the hypersexualization of Black women's bodies and its historical and current consequences.

3. Explore the mammy, strong Black woman, single mother, and other stereotypes of Black women and explore how you have perpetuated them, both in perception and action.

4. Listen to NPR's "Young Black Girls Face 'Adultification'" or read George-town Law's report *Girlhood Interrupted: The Erasure of Black Girls' Childhood* by Rebecca Epstein, Jamilia Blake, and Thalia González.

Identifying as the Empress

How do you already embody the Empress? Use this list of words commonly associated with this card to identify the qualities that you do and don't want to work with as you help create a radically more equitable world.

- Circle the qualities you already embody and can leverage as a superpower.
- Draw a heart around the qualities you want to embody more deeply or frequently.
- Draw a square around the qualities you want to transmute or avoid.

Artistic	Takes responsibility	Realistic	Connected to nature	Rigid
Takes breaks	Sociable	Altruistic	Impatient	Selfish
Avoids change	Cooperative	Communicates openly	Codependent	Supportive
Smothering	Productive	Listens	Jealous	Hoards

Affirmations for Embodying the Empress

As you step into the hopeful realm of the Empress, you might choose an affirmation to motivate you when the work is difficult. Affirmations can strengthen commitment by supporting your confidence in achieving personal and community goals. They can also help combat fear, anxiety, self-doubt, and loss of motivation, which are common feelings that come up in social justice work. You can chant them, write them down, meditate on them, add them to your phone background, or otherwise work with them consistently to keep focused on your objectives. Here are some examples.

"I am inherently creative."

"My actions matter because I am infinitely interconnected."

"Every day, I give birth to myself."

"I'm brave enough to create and I'm humble enough to grow."

"Knowing when to rest is a superpower."

✎ **Often, the most powerful affirmations are the ones we create for ourselves. Take some time to jot down your personal affirmations.**

Magical Practices to Conjure the Empress

Find out where your water comes from. Decolonize outdoors culture. Make sense of your dreams. Start a community refrigerator. Evaluate your culture's beauty standards and how you uphold them. Keep track of the rhythms present in the movements you're a part of. Offer creative coaching or outlets to under-served people. Be gentle with yourself so you can be bold. Increase and protect abortion access. Leave your prejudiced partner. Lead with soft power. Make sure organizations focus on both progress and sustainable maintenance.

Becoming the Empress

Meditate on your relationship with the Empress and use what you know to plan real-world action. By responding to these prompts, you are committing to doing the work—period.

SET A PERSONAL, RELATIONAL, OR COLLECTIVE INTENTION

✎ **Name an objective that your work will center around.**

✎ **Plan specific actions for this objective that you will take as you embody the Empress.**

✎ This [day/week/month/event], I will embody the Empress in my liberation work by

_____

✎ This work is important because _____

✎ The affirmation I will repeat is _____

REFLECT ON YOUR EXPERIENCE

✎ Evolution is iterative and often nonlinear. As we pursue our goals, we must regularly evaluate our actions, mistakes, and learnings to inform the next cycles of change. Review your experience and identify what you can take with you as you move through your antiracism work.

- Successes
- Setbacks
- Frustrations
- Questions
- Other reflections
- Next steps

BUILDING A TOOLKIT

Defend Public Spaces

The Empress protects their garden because they know its value. For some, it's a place of respite. For others, it's a source of sustenance. Their garden is *in* the world and thus it is *of* the world—none of their gardening is truly isolated.

The Empress's fertility is visible in public spaces, such as parks and community centers. These are places for celebrations, social exchanges, and cross-cultural interactions. They contribute to community health socially, culturally, economically, and environmentally. Public spaces build and fortify communities and when they disappear, the people who relied on them can experience isolation and decreased sense of responsibility for community care.

Increasingly, public spaces are decimated for profit. A bingo hall becomes a fast fashion store; the park with a view becomes home to fancy housing developments. Communities of color are more likely to be affected by such enclosure. Reflect on the value of public spaces in your neighborhood or city; then ideate ways to protect them from industrialization, greed, and pollution.

What are some public community spaces near you?

How do these spaces benefit the community?

What does access to these spaces look like?

How do you and the people you know engage with these spaces?

How might increased privatization show up in your community?

How has increased privatization already shown up in your community?

What are the effects of privatization on marginalized people in your community?

How can you help preserve public spaces, particularly for BIPOC?

How can you help create safe spaces for BIPOC in your community?

Describe how your town's zoning processes have impacted oppressed groups.

What tools and policies does your local government use to defend its zoning decisions?

In a more ideal world, how would you direct your local government on how to approach development in more equitable ways? How can you integrate these strategies into your antiracism work?

4

THE EMPEROR

When I dare to be powerful, to use my strength in the service of my vision, then it becomes less and less important whether I am afraid.

—AUDRE LORDE

The Emperor leverages the Empress's raw creative energy to strategize and build sustainable structures that deliver results. Outlined by the Earth in Aries, they give form to creative ideas. In other words, this archetype makes the work practical. They see the world they want to live in; then they produce it. They have to: if they don't take advantage of their power, someone else will.

This archetype stands between the Empress's big picture views and the Hierophant's focus on details. But the Emperor isn't just zooming in and out all the time. Simultaneously, they consider overarching goals and everyday, mundane tasks. Focusing too heavily on the big picture, they lose sight of the actual tasks needed to make things happen. Excessively scrutinizing details, they lose sight of their overall purpose.

As key four, the Emperor confronts and evaluates structures. They analyze their mental constructs that perpetuate bias. They analyze the constructs in their relationships that perpetuate oppression. They analyze societal constructs that facilitate harm and must be destroyed.

The Emperor is often depicted as a leader, but a more fitting description would be "someone who holds space for the collective." They do so through discipline and restraint, not overcontrol. They listen to others' needs and place them ahead of their own selfish motivations. They're not here for a crown; they're here for a new world.

The Emperor is secure enough in their personal power to confront authority. They watch how people rise to societal power and how others defer to those authorities. By learning processes like government elections, they design strategies to subvert the oppressive elements that deny access and equity to underserved people. The Emperor learns the rules so they can find out how to break them.

Despite knowing their power, the Emperor persistently demonstrates restraint. They know what they have control over and they know when to share or relinquish control when someone else is better suited for the job. They pass the mic. They're no better or worse than any of their comrades; they lean into their unique knack for constructing spaces where people have opportunities to step into their distinctively inherent power for a greater good.

The Emperor can

- Exhibit dependability and stability
- Be a go-getter
- Approach conflict rationally
- Know when to delegate
- Teach others how to harness their power
- Serve as an event planner, dominatrix, accountant, carpenter, or engineer

Embodied Keywords

Pull out the Emperor card from one deck or several. Take a deep breath and pause. Gaze at the imagery. From a liberation perspective, envision yourself in the card's landscape. Be the archetype. Name some keywords that you personally associate with this card. Remember, your definitions are more relevant to your tarot reading than what's in the little white book. Here are a few keywords to help get you started.

> Foundation, logic, management, reliable, collective, construction and deconstruction, planning, strategy, ambition, organization, holding space, productivity, math, surveillance, inner strength, commitment, confidence

Your keywords: _____

The Emperor in Liberation Work

The Emperor claims their power boldly. They know their skill set and how they can employ their privilege to improve access to new and existing societal structures. Because they own their personal power, they are responsible for it. The Emperor periodically evaluates themselves to ensure they're not absentmindedly abusing their power. They also remain open to others' perspectives. Everyone has blind spots, and the Emperor intentionally provides ways others can share unfiltered feedback.

The Emperor stimulates. Led by experience, their leadership is both inspiring and grounded in reality. They've done the work, and now they scale their efforts by encouraging people to do the same. Power only goes so far when it is held by just one person or group. The Emperor gives speeches, organizes protests, starts petitions, balances budgets, and helps others realize their power to effect change. They don't just recline while everyone else works. They continue to do the work because their efforts create blueprints that others can follow or transform. The Emperor walks it like they talk it.

This archetype bucks the patriarchy in novel ways. They realize that the patriarchy extends far beyond white men in power, that it is deeply embedded in our community structures, language, relationships, expectations, and organizing strategies. With discipline and regardless of gender, the Emperor leads by example to demonstrate what leadership without patriarchy can look like.

The Emperor builds because what they want doesn't exist. They're trailblazers. They resonate with what Audre Lorde said about creating new worlds:

> For the master's tools will never dismantle the master's house. They may allow us temporarily to beat him at his own game, but they will never enable us to bring about genuine change.

The Emperor thoughtfully writes new blueprints informed by the successes and failures of previous endeavors.

Correspondences for Inspiration

Consider exploring sources of inspiration that you associate with the Emperor. To help get you started, here are a few popular correspondences.

> Owls, hawks, eagles, silverback gorillas, rams, bloodroot, geranium, oak, sight, myrrh, basil, cinnamon, dragon's blood, topaz, diamond, red jasper, topaz, carnelian, bridges, beaver dams

✎ **What reminds you of the Emperor? How do these things inspire you to keep going?**

How the Emperor Can Show Up

There are as many interpretations of tarot as there are people who have ever lived. There is no completely universal card interpretation because there is no completely universal perspective on life. Your and your clients' interpretations are what matter the most during a reading. Of all the possible magical ingredients, we humans are the most powerful in enacting real-world change. However, there are strong collective energies around the themes that appear more frequently when a particular archetype shows up. Here are some of those common motifs.

THE BALANCED EMPEROR

- Leads with grace
- Amplifies others' voices
- Shares responsibility
- Is practical and methodical
- Inspires
- Shows reliability
- Keeps promises
- Has a clear plan

✎ **My relationship to the Emperor feels balanced when** _____

- Controls
- Set on doing things the way they've always been done
- Hesitant to delegate
- Is narcissistic
- Scared to escape structures that hold them back
- Manipulates people
- Always has the loudest voice in the room

My relationship to the Emperor feels imbalanced when _____

Deconstructing the Language of Othering

The topic of language often arises with the Chariot, but it also fits well with the Emperor because it's a tool that provides structure and boundaries to concepts so we can communicate them beyond ourselves. We might think about how language on a larger scale, such as mass media, perpetuates structural racism, but what about our everyday language? What about the language you use with the people you know? And what about the language you use with yourself when you perceive your world?

Before moving on, meditate on the following prompts:

- Intentionally or unintentionally, have you ever assigned positive or negative attributes to Black people you have seen or encountered in person?

- Intentionally or unintentionally, have you ever expected a Black person to speak as a representative of their race?

- Intentionally or unintentionally, have you ever used certain language due to being distrustful of Black people?

- Intentionally or unintentionally, have you ever thought or talked of Black people as being less intelligent or skilled?

- Intentionally or unintentionally, have you unnecessarily mentioned someone's Blackness when speaking about them (e.g., "I met a guy at the coffee shop" vs. "I met a Black guy at the coffee shop")?

- Consider how you enforce Blackness as "the other" in your language.

Large, rapidly evolving societies tend to create rules around who gets to be a full member of society and who doesn't, a process known as "othering." The folks at Othering and Belonging define the term as

> A set of dynamics, processes, and structures that engender marginality and persistent inequality across any of the full range of human differences based on group identities. Thirteen dimensions of othering include, but are not limited to, religion, sex, race, ethnicity, socioeconomic status (class), disability, sexual orientation, and skin tone. Although the axes of difference that undergird these expressions of othering vary considerably and are deeply contextual, they contain a similar set of underlying dynamics.

Othering goes beyond whether we like someone or whether we're aware of a person's presence. It's a conscious and unconscious mindset, positioning a certain group as having less belonging in a socially or societally favored group through bias, ignorance, and accepted language. Not surprisingly, the concept of "the other" is typically embodied by groups of people that one doesn't personally interface with. Social codes uphold othering by identifying traits the privileged group defines as normal.

What is the structure that determines who gets to be "we" and who gets to be "they"?

The answer isn't the same for every place all the time. Yet, anti-Blackness is global, and it's worth identifying who the Other is in your community, coven, household, or friend group. No group of people is a monolith, and that includes the Black community.

It is easy to overlook someone's humanity when you can't distinguish them from another person.

Nothing about the stories we tell ourselves is unchangeable.

Nothing about our beliefs and biases is unchangeable.

Nothing about our feelings is unchangeable.

Nothing about our awareness of language is unchangeable.

Nothing about our use of language is unchangeable.

So who is "we" and who is "they"? And what is the bridge between the two? The goal of freeing oppressed people isn't to turn the Other into the Same, but to include. We can be both different and inclusive. White people can not only invite Black people to the function, but involve them meaningfully without judging or ignoring their race. The words we use now are foundational to the way we'll communicate, interact, and view each other in our new world. How will you start adjusting yours?

SUGGESTED EXERCISES

1. Read the poem "Sympathy" by Paul Laurence Dunbar.

2. Research the negative impacts of African American Vernacular English (AAVE) exploitation and digital blackface.

3. Listen to Nina Simone's "Mississippi Goddam" and think about the meaning behind the refrain "do it slow."

4. Explore language as a structure of oppression and plan to respond by shifting at least three ways you use language with others.

5. If you are a content creator, check out the Conscious Style Guide or sign up for their free monthly newsletter.

6. Read Toni Morrison's book *The Origin of Others*.

Identifying as the Emperor

How do you already embody the Emperor? Use this list of words commonly associated with this card to identify the qualities that you do and don't want to work with as you help create a radically more equitable world.

- Circle the qualities you already embody and can leverage as a superpower.
- Draw a heart around the qualities you want to embody more deeply or frequently.
- Draw a square around the qualities you want to transmute or avoid.

Leader	Active listener	Disciplined	Aloof	Accountable
Afraid to speak up	Involved	Manifestor	Disorganized	Ambitious
Lazy	Practical	Protector	Authoritative	Interrupts people
Notices patterns	Seeks truth	Self-absorbed	Strategic	Distant

Affirmations for Embodying the Emperor

As you step into the hopeful realm of the Emperor, you might choose an affirmation to motivate you when the work is difficult. Affirmations can strengthen commitment by supporting your confidence in achieving personal and community goals. They can also help combat fear, anxiety, self-doubt, and loss of motivation, which are common feelings that come up in social justice work. You can chant them, write them down, meditate on them, add them to your phone background, or otherwise work with them consistently to keep focused on your objectives. Here are some examples.

"If I don't use my power, someone else will."

"Power with, not power over."

"I lead by conscious example."

"I fuel my community because I am fueled by my community."

"I hold space like I hold my heart."

✎ Often, the most powerful affirmations are the ones we create for ourselves. Take some time to jot down your personal affirmations.

Magical Practices to Conjure the Emperor

Find initiatives you can colead. Make budgets. Revisit your why. Develop confidence. Investigate your relationship with authority. Create a launch plan. Elevate others. Delegate tasks. Identify your talents and how you can use them to inspire. Brainstorm tangible solutions. Prioritize your efforts with external input. Embody qualities of other social justice leaders. Make sure your actions clearly relate back to specific goals. Stand up to established figures. Practice boundary work. Build morale. Analyze your movement's impact and plan how you can be even more effective.

Becoming the Emperor

Meditate on your relationship with the Emperor and use what you know to plan real-world action. By responding to these prompts, you are committing to doing the work—period.

SET A PERSONAL, RELATIONAL, OR COLLECTIVE INTENTION

✎ Name an objective that your work will center around.

✎ Plan specific actions for this objective that you will take as you embody the Emperor.

✎ This [day/week/month/event], I will embody the Emperor in my liberation work by

_____

✎ This work is important because _____

✎ The affirmation I will repeat is _____

REFLECT ON YOUR EXPERIENCE

✎ Evolution is iterative and often nonlinear. As we pursue our goals, we must regularly evaluate our actions, mistakes, and learnings to inform the next cycles of change. Review your experience and identify what you can take with you as you move through your antiracism work.

- Successes

- Setbacks

- Frustrations

- Questions

- Other reflections

- Next steps

Encourage Workplace Equity

For many of us, our jobs create structures in society and in our everyday lives. The Emperor approaches structures with an analytical eye: they survey the landscape and use their observations to determine how to act. Consider how your workplace reinforces or disrupts supremacy culture; then decide how you will change how you show up to work.

What is your company's mission statement?

How does the percentage of Black employees at your company compare to the percentage of Black people in your community?

What is the racial makeup of your company's leadership?

How are you an ally to coworkers from marginalized groups?

How do you give or support opportunities for nonwhite people to lead, get their voices heard, and move up the career ladder?

How has your company addressed racism?

What racial issues currently exist in your company?

How does racism obstruct your nonwhite colleagues' careers?

How has your company acknowledged Black Lives Matter?

How do respectability politics show up in your workplace? How do expectations of professionalism reinforce white supremacy?

Which colleagues are antiracist allies and advocates?

What does pay equity look like at your workplace?

What are your coworkers' salaries?

How can you support pay equity at your workplace?

What structures for change exist in your company?

How is your company actively antiracist, beyond bandaids and rhetoric?

Is your company publicly vocal about its diversity efforts?

Does your company participate in local diversity, equity, and inclusion (DEI)?

Does your company speak about DEI efforts specifically or generally? Is the language they use unique or does it sound templatized?

Does your organization's DEI strategy list and publicize clear, actionable plans?

Who is involved in DEI efforts? What does the overall engagement look like?

How does your company measure DEI progress?

How is your company's recruitment process inclusive?

How is your company's hiring process inclusive?

How does your company identify the right people for specific jobs?

What does an anti-oppressive interview process look like? How does this compare to interviews at your company?

How do other companies meaningfully approach antiracism?

In the name of racial liberation, how will you participate in uncomfortable work situations?

How will you be braver at work going forward?

5

THE HIEROPHANT

When you believe niceness disproves the presence of racism, it's easy to start believing bigotry is rare, and that the label racist should be applied only to mean-spirited, intentional acts of discrimination. The problem with this framework—besides being a gross misunderstanding of how racism operates in systems and structures enabled by nice people—is that it obligates me to be nice in return, rather than truthful.

—AUSTIN CHANNING BROWN

The Hierophant is at once student and teacher, descendant and ancestor. In Rider-Waite-Smith-based tarot decks, key five is often the first time we witness an exchange between two people. The Hierophant is an intersection, a crossroads. They stand between the past and the future as they learn, integrate, and teach at the same time. Their knowledge of the past enlightens their faith in the future, the faith that what they do today delivers results tomorrow. The benevolent Hierophant is what Layla Saad describes as a "good ancestor."

The Hierophant is a nonconformist who examines their beliefs deeply and critically. They ask "What?" but they also ask "Why?" They're persistent in their mission to uncover hidden truths about their worlds to answer the question of how we got here. This is a card of ancestry, of lineages. The Hierophant is daring enough to get real about how their ancestors, living and passed on, have perpetuated racial oppression publicly and privately. When they explore the roots of their beliefs, they ask, "Who are my conscious and subconscious teachers?" The answers pinpoint the traditions to continue and the ones to break free from. They're ready to do things differently.

Discovering uncomfortable truths can present significant challenges to the Hierophant. Its number five is one of conflict and tension in the name of growth. Evolution is sometimes painful. Yet the Hierophant continues the work. They explore their resistance to change and define what it means for their social justice work. Their lessons transform them forever. The Hierophant is never the same person before and after didactic experiences.

Illustrated by Mercury in Taurus, the Hierophant's learning is deliberate. Through Taurus's patience, subtle strength, and practicality, Mercury intellectually processes questions through the subconscious and sends the analysis back to the conscious mind to inform action. They don't learn only for curiosity's sake. They learn to apply and teach. The Hierophant is a channel between the questions and the answers. They share their knowledge, inspiring students to build upon it and identify what authentically aligns with their antiracism journeys.

Because the Hierophant has seen the past, they have faith in the future. The Hierophant can

- Be open-minded
- Recognize times to defy tradition
- Seek learning opportunities
- Dedicate themselves to continual evolution
- Archive their lessons for others to learn from
- Serve as a bookkeeper, religious leader, philosopher, or board member

Embodied Keywords

Pull out the Hierophant card from one deck or several. Take a deep breath and pause. Gaze at the imagery. From a liberation perspective, envision yourself in the card's landscape. Be the archetype. Name some keywords that you personally associate with this card. Remember, your definitions are more relevant to your tarot reading than what's in the little white book. Here are a few keywords to help get you started.

Group mentality, tradition, challenge, education, beliefs, societal institutions, ancestry, mentorship, faith, curiosity, meeting students where they are, processing and disseminating information, intersections, evolution, growing pains

Your keywords: _____

The Hierophant in Liberation Work

One of the Hierophant's priorities is remaining teachable. They use their awareness of the status quo to decide precedents to follow and rules to break. They mind others' footprints and won't recreate the wheel if they don't have to. At the same time, they're prepared to carve unfamiliar paths that make the work more effective, relevant, and scalable.

The Hierophant is a tenacious advocate for collective learning. They might lead onboarding sessions, teach relevant organizing strategies, or facilitate antibias training for companies. They remain aware of their students' backgrounds and current knowledge so they can meet them where they are. They specifically curate their lessons for their audiences because the information they share must be clear and relevant in order to do something with it. The Hierophant's message is useless if the receivers don't understand it.

The Hierophant inspires people to identify what is true for them and their communities. They get people to exit autopilot mode to question their beliefs and face difficult truths. As a result, people reconsider their everyday actions, including where they shop, how they interact with others, the rhetoric they use, their fixations, and the systems they use to cultivate more inclusive communities.

This archetype knows who their teachers are. They study a diverse array of sources and regularly audit their sources of information. They name and research their teachers, clean up their social media feeds, stay on top of their news sources, and critically review how their teachers' environments and cultures shaped their lessons. They don't accept information at face value—they investigate information even when they're used to trusting certain sources.

The Hierophant maintains archives. They're both past-aware and future-focused, considering documentation like writings and oral histories to uncover what has and hasn't worked in the past. They try not to repeat prior mistakes, as they view every situation as a chance to learn or reinforce useful information. Careful not to homogenize their information sources, the Hierophant elevates voices often silenced by white supremacy. They craft stages for people to learn from diverse backgrounds and experiences. For example, they might get their neighbors to learn about housing discrimination by hearing from unhoused people in their district. They find perspectives from their communities and, with permission, elevate them to inspire and inform movements.

Correspondences for Inspiration

Consider exploring sources of inspiration that you associate with the Hierophant. To help get you started, here are a few popular correspondences.

> Tigers, bulls, polar bears, white cranes, elephants, sage, hawthorn, lily of the valley, vervain, mallow, ears, voice, storax, costus, garnet, sapphire, jade, topaz

✎ What reminds you of the Hierophant? How do these things inspire you to keep going?

How the Hierophant Can Show Up

There are as many interpretations of tarot as there are people who have ever lived. There is no completely universal card interpretation because there is no completely universal perspective on life. Your and your clients' interpretations are what matter the most during a reading. Of all the possible magical ingredients, we humans are the most powerful in enacting real-world change. However, there are strong collective energies around the themes that appear more frequently when a particular archetype shows up. Here are some of those common motifs.

THE BALANCED HIEROPHANT

- Understanding
- Elevates diverse perspectives
- Retains knowledge

- Notices historical patterns
- Knows their unique teaching skills
- Learns from elders
- Commits to mental evolution

My relationship to the Hierophant feels balanced when _____

THE IMBALANCED HIEROPHANT

- Constrained by rules
- Dogmatic
- Runs on autopilot
- Gives in easily to societal expectations
- Pressures others to think like they do
- Evangelizes insensitively
- Doesn't practice what they preach

My relationship to the Hierophant feels imbalanced when _____

Remaining Committed Around Problematic Family

The Hierophant mirrors our faith in various aspects of our lives and our selves. Experience helps us develop faith in our learning and growth, our intuition, our curiosity, and the lenses we apply. We also develop faith in each other. In *The Tarot Handbook,* Angeles Arrien writes of this archetype, "Metaphorically, this symbol represents our capacity and need to learn how to walk the mystical path with practical feet. The Hierophant is that part of ourselves that knows how to directly apply the sacred, that is within all of us, to the outer world."

This figure can raise themes around faith, learning, conformity and noncon-formity, cultivating and honoring (and changing) traditions, and examining the institutions in our personal and public lives.

The Hierophant's depiction in the Thoth deck features a being, the initiator (#1), surrounded by four creatures (#2–5). These symbols represent gifts that we can apply to any of our work, including our racial justice efforts:

The eagle represents Scorpio, a symbol of loyalty, deep passion, and commitment.

The human face represents Aquarius, a symbol of fearless pioneering, unique ideas, and futuristic thinking.

The lion represents Leo, a symbol of boundless, expansive creativity.

The bull represents Taurus, a symbol of bringing our ideas into tangible form.

It's worth noting that these symbols are the fixed signs of the zodiac, suggesting that the work we do, that which is grounded in our faith for the future, must be sustainable, stable, deep, persistent, and determined. Meditate upon each symbol for a few moments, thinking about how each one uniquely fits into the work you do every single day to shatter structural racism.

Consider applying the Hierophant's inspiration in your work by thinking about Mercury in Taurus: grounded, practical communication—the exchange of ideas.

This brings me to another one of the Hierophant's themes: family, and how they can test our convictions and devotion.

Turn your lens toward your family, biological or otherwise.

For many white people, confronting their family's racism is where the going gets rough. It's the final frontier of their discomfort, and only those who may enter are those willing to disavow ways their loved ones contribute to the global oppression, violence, and murder of nonwhite people.

"That's just who they are."

"I can't disown my family."

"I don't want to hurt my relationship with my mom."

"We just don't talk about it."

"We agree to disagree about anything political."

"They'll never change, so what's the point?"

"They don't know how to talk without arguing, so I just avoid it."

"Doesn't my public work cancel out my relationship with my parents?"

If you've said any of these things about your racist family (or otherwise over-looked their oppression to keep the peace), are you not an accomplice to their racism?

Many white people call racism out everywhere but in their own homes. The avoidance of rocking the boat is vital to the continuance of racial oppression. The Hierophant encourages us to examine that which led us to where we are and the expectations around where we should be going and then to seek the knowledge to discern whether that path is the one we should follow or step away from. If you've abandoned your family's racist traditions, then you've already made one move off that generational path. Yet this work doesn't exist solely within you and your own belief system—it must reach beyond.

I spoke to some people about their strategies to confront racist beliefs and language with their family.

> I had to go into it [the conversation] knowing that it would be really hard. That took a lot of effort to just kind of sit with. I hate confrontation, but I felt more prepared after I accepted that fact. It also helped me to practice how I could calm myself down with breathing because I can't think straight when I'm feeling so anxious and I always just want to shut down.

> One thing that helped them understand where I was coming from was just explaining the realizations and experiences I had that led me to the work I'm doing now.

> I brought a list, a literal list, of ways that my family has white privilege. I don't know if they were convinced all of them were true, but it at least got the conversation started in a more personal way.

> Naming out the concrete ways that they could literally impact their communities by changing their ways made it more real for us.

> I prepared by thinking of example situations of how racism affects Black and Brown people so I could use them with [my family]. They don't listen when I tell them they're being racist when they say something shitty, but illustrating how their actions are

harmful in the real world opens up a dialogue. It doesn't always end well, but I'm still trying.

I don't make it all about me. I ask questions that get them talking and lead to back-and-forth conversations. I try not to cut them off when I'm getting angry, I just listen and then respond when it's my turn. I think they appreciate knowing that I'm serious and I'm seriously valuing them as conversational partners.

My family's pretty insular, so talking about stuff that happens a thousand miles away will never work. So I try to connect the things that are happening in our town and county with broader implications of systemic oppression.

After a certain point, I just had to set up some harsh boundaries between the people in my family who just wouldn't listen. It felt bad, but I had to do it. They need to know I'm serious.

These conversations with people you love dearly aren't often easy, but they're imperative. We should act as though we constantly reverberate beyond ourselves, toward the people closest to us and our effect through them, and then the people they interact with, and so on. We can leave marks on people we'll never meet. You're not only charged with remaining teachable, but also with teaching as you learn. You are the most primed to reach the people closest to you. And if that doesn't work, well, you could just break up with them.

SUGGESTED EXERCISES

1. Listen to, or read, NPR's "Want to Have Better Conversations About Racism with Your Parents? Here's How."

2. Watch The Lily's "Why You Need to Keep Talking About Race with Your White Family."

3. Read "Dear Fellow White People: Here's What to Do When You're Called Racist" by Rebecca Hains.

4. Review UMN's "Examples of Racial Microaggressions" list. Then think about the times you have heard these in your close circles. Why haven't you

always spoken up? How can you make sure to be an ally in these situations going forward?

5. Read *Beyond Your Bubble: How to Connect Across the Political Divide, Skills and Strategies for Conversations That Work* by Tania Israel.

Identifying as the Hierophant

How do you already embody the Hierophant? Use this list of words commonly associated with this card to identify the qualities that you do and don't want to work with as you help create a radically more equitable world.

- Circle the qualities you already embody and can leverage as a superpower.
- Draw a heart around the qualities you want to embody more deeply or frequently.
- Draw a square around the qualities you want to transmute or avoid.

Has faith	Resists change	Considers diverse sources	Traditional	Critical thinker
Listens to firsthand experiences	Open-minded	Unwilling to look at own flaws	Repairs ancestral harm	Hopeful
Messenger	Creates real-world applications	Mentor	Communicates clearly	Formal
Aware	Enthusiastic about learning	Inflexible	Observant	Rebellious

Affirmations for Embodying the Hierophant

As you step into the hopeful realm of the Hierophant, you might choose an affirmation to motivate you when the work is difficult. Affirmations can strengthen commitment by supporting your confidence in achieving personal and community goals. They can also help combat fear, anxiety, self-doubt, and loss of motivation, which are common feelings that come up in social justice work. You can chant them, write them down, meditate on them, add them to your phone background, or otherwise work with them consistently to keep focused on your objectives. Here are some examples.

"Everything is a teacher."

"I will learn one new thing today."

"My faith is a verb."

"I'm ready to pivot when I learn new information."

"I am both teacher and student."

 Often, the most powerful affirmations are the ones we create for ourselves. Take some time to jot down your personal affirmations.

Magical Practices to Conjure the Hierophant

Analyze historical movements. Learn from diverse sources in your physical and online communities. Host productive discourse. Identify tensions in your anti-racism work. Confront internalized racism. End each day by reflecting on lessons learned. List your teachers and define why you choose them. Start a blog. Call out your friends' racism. Facilitate storytelling events. Elicit advice from people who know more than you do. Join a social group for change. Identify inequities in your community's schools and devise plans to increase educational access.

Becoming the Hierophant

Meditate on your relationship with the Hierophant and use what you know to plan real-world action. By responding to these prompts, you are committing to doing the work—period.

SET A PERSONAL, RELATIONAL, OR COLLECTIVE INTENTION

 Name an objective that your work will center around.

✎ Plan specific actions for this objective that you will take as you embody the Hierophant.

✎ This [day/week/month/event], I will embody the Hierophant in my liberation work by _____

✎ This work is important because _____

✎ The affirmation I will repeat is _____

REFLECT ON YOUR EXPERIENCE

✎ Evolution is iterative and often nonlinear. As we pursue our goals, we must regularly evaluate our actions, mistakes, and learnings to inform the next cycles of change. Review your experience and identify what you can take with you as you move through your antiracism work.

- Successes
- Setbacks
- Frustrations
- Questions
- Other reflections
- Next steps

Let the Past Enlighten Tomorrow

The Hierophant gazes into the past to create a vision for the future. List five activists and disruptors that have inspired you and describe how their experiences inform your current work.

Person(s): _____

How they influence my work: _____

Person(s): _____

How they influence my work: _____

Person(s): _____

How they influence my work: _____

Person(s): _____

How they influence my work: _____

Person(s): _____

How they influence my work: _____

6

THE LOVERS

Outside of right and wrong, there is a field. I'll meet you there.

—RUMI

Before the Lovers align, they make the embodied decision to conjoin. They advocate that love is a choice as much as it is an action. This card can appear when the querent has options beyond their current conscious awareness. Though many illustrations depict this archetype with a man and a woman, the Lovers card can actually queer the idea of love. Love moves through countless forms and thus goes beyond any binary.

The Lovers are a picture of deep listening that fosters genuine partnerships. They're confident that their impact is more powerful when they join forces with other people. They've learned that relating to other people can tell them a lot about themselves. Through the other, they recognize their true selves. And thus, the Lovers also conjure the relationship with the self. The Lovers lend a mirror to us that reflects images of ourselves framed by the people around us. The Lovers inspire us to show up as we'd like others to show up for us and the collective.

The Venusian Lovers are values driven. They know the core beliefs that drive their work, their everyday decisions that build the world to come. They move with authentic integrity and willfully traverse between their wants and their responsibilities. Sometimes those things align and other times they do not. The Lovers consult their evolving values to make responsible choices when caught between desire or convenience and the right thing to do.

The Lovers celebrate the differences between people. They see how people are in their movements and how they uniquely contribute to shared causes. It takes many kinds of people to make the world go around, so the Lovers don't dictate rigid expectations of how others must act. The Lovers' world isn't black and white. They hang out in the gray area where their collaborators' efforts are no more or less worthwhile than theirs. The Lovers appreciate their partners' individual differences because they cultivate empathy, expand their overall mission, and help develop more inclusive futures.

The Lovers can

- Use interactions to fuel their work
- Recognize and control selfish motivations
- Make energetic space for genuine connections with comrades
- Practice diplomacy
- Have clear values
- Believe that love comes in many forms
- Serve as a counselor, multimedia artist, public relations specialist, or customer service representative

Embodied Keywords

Pull out the Lovers card from one deck or several. Take a deep breath and pause. Gaze at the imagery. From a liberation perspective, envision yourself in the card's landscape. Be the archetype. Name some keywords that you personally associate with this card. Remember, your definitions are more relevant to your tarot reading than what's in the little white book. Here are a few keywords to help get you started.

Unions, choices, sharing, community building, embracing diversity, passion, devotion, ethics, listening, shared investments, interactions, harmony, safety, telling things apart, balance, being present, magnetism, compromise, coleadership

✎ **Your keywords:** _____

The Lovers in Liberation Work

The Lovers find strength in community. They don't just notice others' unique qualities. The Lovers regularly help people recognize these traits within themselves and embolden people to use their skills in ways that complement the larger mission. The Lovers makes connections, and that means reassuring people that they are connected to something bigger than themselves. The Lovers aren't too shy to applaud others' endeavors and energy.

The Lovers are decision-makers who prepare to make trade-offs. Their ethics guide their choices, but not just for themselves. They ensure that their comrades' work reflects community values. The intrepid Lovers involve themselves in generating mission statements and holding others accountable to team agreements. They get people to see that their actions are intricately bonded to the rest of the world. The Lovers are flexible enough to know that values can show up in divergent ways depending on context, including cultures, environments, relationships, and current events.

The gray area is a familiar space for the Lovers. They're the bridge, the connector, the negotiator. Their astute listening skills catalyze meaningful connections. Through these relationships, they see that there is no single path to liberation. The Lovers take note of similarities and differences between various initiatives to determine how groups can cohesively approach community action.

Correspondences for Inspiration

Consider exploring sources of inspiration that you connect with the Lovers. To help get you started, here are a few popular associations.

Magpies, hybrid species, orchids, nut-bearing trees, twins, sense of smell, wormwood, bergamot, lavender, agate, rose quartz, tourmaline, jasmine, harps, knots, maple leaves, swans, confluences

What reminds you of the Lovers? How do these things inspire you to keep going?

How the Lovers Can Show Up

There are as many interpretations of tarot as there are people who have ever lived. There is no completely universal card interpretation because there is no completely universal perspective on life. Your and your clients' interpretations are what matter the most during a reading. Of all the possible magical ingredients, we humans are the most powerful in enacting real-world change. However, there are strong collective energies around the themes that appear more frequently when a particular archetype shows up. Here are some of those common motifs.

THE BALANCED LOVERS

- Value connection
- Take advantage of shared interests
- Listen intentionally
- Bring people together
- Mediate disagreements
- Notice how biases affect their personal relationships
- Show passion and zest

✎ **My relationship to the Lovers feels balanced when** _____

THE IMBALANCED LOVERS

- Fail to humanize others
- Project onto others
- Avoid responsibility
- Struggle with inner conflicts
- Impulsive
- Unethical
- Compromise others' safety

✎ **My relationship to the Lovers feels imbalanced when** _____

Choosing to Redistribute Wealth

After expanding our knowledge, we realize that the world isn't so black and white. There are more than two choices; there is even more than one spectrum—yes, the full landscape is unquantifiable and encompasses more than duality and spectrums.

A common Lovers keyword is "discrimination": the ability to separate different things in order to see the similarities and differences between them. When we can tell things apart, we can choose what to fuse together, leave alone, or abandon.

Some early Tarot decks named the Lovers card "Choice." (Some decks still do!) In equity work, this card arises in many forms, often shaped by our everyday choices. Our work frequently requires us to discriminate between convenience and devotion—to see the potential effects of picking one versus the other and then decide what to do next.

Of course, the Lovers card also suggests the topic of love. Our daily choices that support an antiracist future are examples of love manifest. This work is love on a micro and macro scale. And interpersonal love requires some healthy ego dissolution to collaborate toward equity.

So heed the choices you make each day. More specifically, tune your lens on where you spend your money. Many white people support antiracism but become defensive about their economic power and how they use it.

We may think about choices as a "this or that" or a "one or the other" reductive binary, but we can make choices beyond what we've ever done or experienced.

Unfortunately, capital is power in many white-dominant societies. Generational oppression, gatekeeping, redlining, and other abuses still impact the amount of Black capital—the amount of power they have in a capitalist society. If capital is power, then we can redistribute power through our purchasing choices.

Many folks are hesitant to change where they shop, often out of convenience or habit. The revolution is ultimately anticapitalist but challenges us, in the meanwhile, to shift power dynamics in efforts parallel to the destruction of capitalist regimes. Our work requires the massive redistribution of wealth, and we do our part by scrutinizing where our money goes. This doesn't just include one-off spending, such as holiday shopping, but also where you spend your money in the more mundane aspects of life, such as when choosing a repair person or deciding where to bank.

Place a bookmark on this page and go read all six points Green America makes in "6 Reasons to Support Black-Owned Businesses."

Shifting our purchasing can disrupt noxious power dynamics. We elevate and autonomize communities, fight the racial wealth gap, and hold society account-able for their financial choices. Giving more attention to our typical experiences is a spell. Regularly making minor money decisions, such as your go-to coffee spot, is an easy-but powerful repetitive spell against financial injustice.

SUGGESTED EXERCISES

1. Learn about Tulsa's Black Wall Street and its massacre.

2. Read "The Case for Reparations" by Ta-Nehisi Coates.

3. Find PayPals, Venmos, or CashApps of BIPOC and randomly donate money as reparations.

4. Explore gentrification and, if relevant, identify how it has shown up in your local community and its outcomes. Then commit to one thing you will do in opposition.

5. Download Miiriya (iOS; Google Play), an app akin to Amazon and Etsy, where people can conveniently and directly shop from Black-owned busi-nesses in one place.

6. Check out the Official Black Wall Street's directory of Black-owned busi-nesses and shop from at least one retailer.

7. If you're a white practitioner, include reparations as part of your financial model. Incorporate a sliding scale or another method of leveling the playing field for BIPOC.

Identifying as the Lovers

How do you already embody the Lovers? Use this list of words commonly associated with this card to identify the qualities that you do and don't want to work with as you help create a radically more equitable world.

- Circle the qualities you already embody and can leverage as a superpower.
- Draw a heart around the qualities you want to embody more deeply or frequently.
- Draw a square around the qualities you want to transmute or avoid.

Mediator	Passionate	Seeks instant gratification	Lives in one's head	Hesitant to make new connections
Neglects themselves	Focuses on the binary	Chooses intentionally	Brings people together	Uses beliefs to dominate others
Has communication difficulties	Lives their ethics	Keeps in touch with people	Pushover	Encouraging
One-track mind	Decisive	Participates in meetings	Speaks up for others	Has difficulty being present

Affirmations for Embodying the Lovers

As you embody the passionate Lovers, you might choose an affirmation to motivate you when the work is difficult. Affirmations can strengthen commitment by supporting your confidence in achieving personal and community goals. They can also help combat fear, anxiety, self-doubt, and loss of motivation, which are common feelings that come up in social justice work. You can chant them, write them down, meditate on them, add them to your phone background, or otherwise work with them consistently to keep focused on your objectives. Here are some examples.

"Love is an action."

"I build meaningful connections."

"I'm a part of something greater than myself."

"I live my values."

"I choose what's right over what feels comfortable."

✎ Often, the most powerful affirmations are the ones we create for ourselves. Take some time to jot down your personal affirmations.

Magical Practices to Conjure the Lovers

Determine your core beliefs and how they influence your work. Do things that your future self will thank you for. Learn conflict resolution skills. Consider other people and what they teach you about yourself. Write a personal mission statement. Discuss antiracism with loved ones. Take care of yourself so you can take care of others. Involve antiracism in everyday choices. Bring people together. Build new connections with people different from you. Practice radical honesty. Protect families. Decolonize your domestic life. Create community events. Increase or shift your responsibilities whenever you get too comfortable.

Becoming the Lovers

Meditate on your relationship with the Lovers and use what you know to plan real-world action. By responding to these prompts, you are committing to doing the work—period.

SET A PERSONAL, RELATIONAL, OR COLLECTIVE INTENTION

✎ Name an objective that your work will center around.

✎ Plan specific actions for this objective that you will take as you embody the Lovers.

✎ This [day/week/month/event], I will embody the Lovers in my liberation work by __

✎ This work is important because _____

✎ The affirmation I will repeat is _____

REFLECT ON YOUR EXPERIENCE

✎ Evolution is iterative and often nonlinear. As we pursue our goals, we must regularly evaluate our actions, mistakes, and learnings to inform the next cycles of change. Review your experience and identify what you can take with you as you move through your antiracism work.

- Successes
- Setbacks
- Frustrations
- Questions
- Other reflections
- Next steps

Recognize Intersections

The Lovers value connection because they regard everything as interconnected. No person is an island, and no person is only one thing. We live our lives at the intersections of multiple identities. Kimberlé Crenshaw coined the term "intersectionality," defining it as "a lens through which you can see where power comes and collides, where it interlocks and intersects. It's not simply that there's a race problem here, a gender problem here, and a class or LGBTQ problem there. Many times that framework erases what happens to people who are subject to all of these things."

Use the following prompts to delve into the topic of intersectionality and elucidate how it shapes your racial liberation work.

- **Define identity.**

- **Define intersectionality.**

- **What does intersectional erasure look like?**

- **List terms that describe you, like trans or Afro-Latina.**

- **How do these traits intersect in the way you interact with the world?**

- **How can paying attention to intersectionality improve your ability to effect change? Give specific examples.**

7

THE CHARIOT

But race is the child of racism, not the father.
—TA-NEHISI COATES

The determined Chariot harnesses self-control and willpower to face challenges head-on, both internally and externally. This is a card of experience and integration. The Rider-Waite-Smith Tarot deck imagery backs these themes. We see the Magician's wand (power), the High Priestess's canopy (protection), the Empress's crown (dominion over creation), the Emperor's armor (boundaries), the Hierophant's two moons (lessons from previous generations), and the Lovers' duality in the double sphinxes (combination of opposing forces). Notice that there are no reins; the Chariot steers with their mind. At the end of the Major Arcana's first line, the Chariot has their bags packed and a mentality primed for the trip from the ego into the subconscious. The Chariot must be wise about what they put in their vehicle. Excessive baggage decelerates and overcomplicates the adventure or road trip. The Chariot leans into ego death, shedding parts of their personality that subvert personal and collective evolution. The number 7 relates to individuation. As such, the Chariot contemplates who they want to be for the world they want to see. They challenge anachronistic modes of thought because old maps won't lead to new places. The Chariot might feel imposter syndrome, but they still commit to embodying the roles they want to inhabit. They might not be a racecar driver yet, but they'll wear the suit every day until it fits.

This archetype is a warrior, vigilant and equipped to encounter difficulty with expertise and rigor. They follow a nascent idea about their next destination, but they regularly revisit what success looks like to ensure an ethically aligned expedition. The Chariot chooses from many roads, adjusting direction and speed based on road conditions. Roadside attractions and fatigue present the risk of distraction. But the Chariot is disciplined enough to continue and always fill their tank well before it runs out. Powerful and energetically conservative, the Chariot's valiant spirit is present in their own reins.

The Chariot can

- Push beyond their comfort zone
- Motivate activists to leverage their personalities as superpowers
- Sacrifice for efficient progress
- Control their impulses
- Be highly motivated
- Sustain useful habits
- Serve as a driver, manager, travel agent, or athlete

Embodied Keywords

Pull out the Chariot card from one deck or several. Take a deep breath and pause. Gaze at the imagery. From a liberation perspective, envision yourself in the card's landscape. Be the archetype. Name some keywords that you personally associate with this card. Remember, your definitions are more relevant to your tarot reading than what's in the little white book. Here are a few keywords to help get you started.

> Personality, behavior, travel, willpower, success, determination, mindset, courage, focus, correcting course, productive anxiety, financial discipline, leveling up, risk-taking, repetition, protection, movement, experience, development

✎ Your keywords: _____

The Chariot in Liberation Work

The Chariot acts because they know they're the only ones who can do the work the way they do in the space where they do it.

This archetype is a strategic project manager, leading the creation of road maps and making sure that teams stay on track. They set checkpoints, plan breaks, lead retrospectives, and invariably articulate justifiable reasons for going off course. They help devise and execute plans (and backup plans) based on needs, timelines, and budgets. The Chariot checks that everyone knows their strengths-based roles in collective efforts. They get the car running; then they keep it running.

The Chariot periodically inspects their available revolutionary tools for relevance and functionality. They ask, "Do the old machines work?" "Do we need new tools and strategies?" and "Do we just need to use them differently or repair them?" It's custom for the Chariot to consult the Hierophant's knowledge of the past to critically evaluate whether existing practices are still applicable.

The Chariot practices "be here now." They remain present to not only their surroundings, but their relationship to their surroundings. On the road to a more equitably accessible future, they're consistently aware of the landscape—the people, policies, cultural contexts, and needs. After all, they must be conscious of these things to effectively steer their vehicle without crashing or overheating. They practice being present through meditation, monotasking, journaling, breathwork, active listening, and other ways of conjuring sensitivity to the now.

Key seven confronts their comfort zones and asks where they can go beyond constraints no longer needed. When their work becomes easy and convenient, they know it's time to get uncomfortable again. Being uncomfortable means facing weaknesses and transforming them into more useful things, like drive and perspective. This discomfort often involves difficult conversations—with other people *and* themselves. What worked then isn't going to work now. The Chariot is determined, acting swiftly and tenaciously to curate their mindset and behavior. The world is never the same twice, and neither are we. We must adjust; we must evolve.

Correspondences for Inspiration

Consider exploring sources of inspiration that you associate with the Chariot. To help get you started, here are a few popular correspondences.

Crabs, sphinxes, horses, beetles, turtles, cypress, lotus, olive, vehicles, speech, labdanum, amber, sapphire, antique silver, chalcedony, cinnamon, rosemary, phoenix, butterflies, spring equinox

✎ **What reminds you of the Chariot? How do these things inspire you to keep going?**

How the Chariot Can Show Up

There are as many interpretations of tarot as there are people who have ever lived. There is no completely universal card interpretation because there is no completely universal perspective on life. Your and your clients' interpretations are what matter the most during a reading. Of all the possible magical ingredients, we humans are the most powerful in enacting real-world change. However, there are strong collective energies around the themes that appear more frequently when a particular archetype shows up. Here are some of those common motifs.

THE BALANCED CHARIOT

- Focused
- Integrates
- Redefines success
- Adventurous
- Aware of self and surroundings
- Reflective
- Organized

✎ **My relationship to the Chariot feels balanced when** _____

THE IMBALANCED CHARIOT

- Chooses the easy route
- Stubborn
- Overly anxious

- Doesn't know when to move on
- Reckless
- Feels like an imposter
- Lacks boundaries

✎ **My relationship to the Chariot feels imbalanced when** _____

Confronting and Subduing Overwhelm

When we look at the Rider-Waite-Smith depiction of the Chariot, we catch a glimpse of a figure sitting upon a vehicle headed by two sphinxes. Yet the figure has no reins for steering. They move forward through their energy, their will. They contently gaze upon the path ahead, assured they already have the necessary resources to go forward. Imagine embodying this aspect of the Chariot in your antiracism work. Ask yourself, "Where are my will and energy ready to go beyond?"

When prompted to go further, people may exclaim, "This is overwhelming!" or "I don't know where to start." These worries are completely valid. Yet, we ought to move through those tensions and keep going. Like the Chariot, you can find where you can more confidently and consistently use your resources and energy to steer your activity toward equity.

So where are you willing to go beyond?

If you're feeling overwhelmed, pick a lane. Choose a field or theme to focus your antiracism work. Teachers might focus their work on the education space. Astrologers might focus their work on spirituality culture. Maybe you have a favorite local institution that could use your assistance. Or you're a hiring manager who can subvert company culture by acquiring more diverse candidates.

Again: if you're feeling overwhelmed, pick a lane.

The Chariot sometimes corresponds to the Moon in Cancer. In the Major Arcana three-line grid, the Chariot rests at the end of the initial exploration of the ego. This is a good time for you to check in with yourself and name what you need to release to move forward. What would make this journey less overwhelming? Then where can you focus your efforts? You can spend a lunation exploring what's next. Where could you go a little faster? A little deeper? A little harder?

Pause and examine who you are, where you are, and what lane you can pursue more passionately.

Find strength in your purpose.

The Chariot informs us that we can do multiple things at once. After all, how could any movement be truly linear in such a highly interrelated world? Keep in mind that you can always take multiple approaches, work concurrently in several lanes, or focus on a new topic when circumstances change.

The Chariot, key seven, corresponds to the sevens in the Minor Arcana, the cards of individuation. These cards see themselves individually against the portrait of humanity. When antiracism work is overwhelming and confusing, we can meditate on how we individualize our journeys by assisting or blocking movement. What can you work through to be more authentic in your work? What's in the way, and how will you move it? How can you focus your lens to generate even more impact?

Yes, you are just one person. Yet the greater movement requires many small efforts.

The Chariot is a warrior card, on macro and micro levels. Where will you fight?

SUGGESTED EXERCISES

1. Explore the White Accomplices' "Opportunities for White People in the Fight for Racial Justice" site. You can also download the complete PDF.

2. Watch "The History of Whiteness" by Kat Blaque.

3. Read "White Privilege Weariness" and "White Privilege Weariness Part 2" by Austin Channing Brown.

4. Check out "Confronting Racism Is Not About the Needs and Feelings of White People" by Ijeoma Oluo.

5. Read *Revolutionary Solidarity* by Pierleone Porcu, Daniela Carmignani, Wolfi Landstreicher, Killing King Abacus, and list several ways that you can be an accomplice in your chosen lane(s).

Identifying as the Chariot

How do you already embody the Chariot? Use this list of words commonly associated with this card to identify the qualities that you do and don't want to work with as you help create a radically more equitable world.

- Circle the qualities you already embody and can leverage as a superpower.

- Draw a heart around the qualities you want to embody more deeply or frequently.

- Draw a square around the qualities you want to transmute or avoid.

Looks ahead	Workaholic	Organized	Reinvents themselves	Shows up, rain or shine
Resigns easily	Hasty	Orderly	Aggressive	Stuck in old habits
Takes breaks	Consistent	Headstrong	Plans	Has self-control
Learns from struggles	Endures	Navigates difficult conversations	Feels protected	Aspirational

Affirmations for Embodying the Chariot

As you align yourself with the Chariot's ambitious nature, you might choose an affirmation to motivate you when the work is difficult. Affirmations can strengthen commitment by supporting your confidence in achieving personal and community goals. They can also help combat fear, anxiety, self-doubt, and loss of motivation, which are common feelings that come up in social justice work. You can chant them, write them down, meditate on them, add them to your phone background, or otherwise work with them consistently to keep focused on your objectives. Here are some examples.

"I am divinely protected."

"As the earth turns, so do I."

"To do, I must try."

"I'm not afraid to change the world."

"I believe in tomorrow, even if I cannot see it."

✏️ Often, the most powerful affirmations are the ones we create for ourselves. Take some time to jot down your personal affirmations.

Magical Practices to Conjure the Chariot

Learn about the societal effects of roads and infrastructure in your community. Increase free access to public transportation. Go to a new place. Identify someone who represents determination and embody their spirit for a week. Reflect and identify strategies and knowledge you can integrate or transform. Realign with your organization's antiracist mission. Perform protection spells. Set up a recurring donation to a meaningful cause. Work in cycles. Notice where ego holds you back. Name your distractions and plan how you will conquer them. Drive people to the polls. Do trance work.

Becoming the Chariot

Meditate on your relationship with the Chariot and use what you know to plan real-world action. By responding to these prompts, you are committing to doing the work—period.

SET A PERSONAL, RELATIONAL, OR COLLECTIVE INTENTION

✏️ Name an objective that your work will center around.

✏️ Plan specific actions for this objective that you will take as you embody the Chariot.

✏️ This [day/week/month/event], I will embody the Chariot in my liberation work by

_____

✎ This work is important because _____

✎ The affirmation I will repeat is _____

REFLECT ON YOUR EXPERIENCE

✎ Evolution is iterative and often nonlinear. As we pursue our goals, we must regularly evaluate our actions, mistakes, and learnings to inform the next cycles of change. Review your experience and identify what you can take with you as you move through your antiracism work.

- Successes
- Setbacks
- Frustrations
- Questions
- Other reflections
- Next steps

Advocate for Migrants

The Chariot personifies figurative and literal travel. Many of us live within or alongside significant migrant populations that endure nationalistic resistance. Xenophobia is often a white supremacist tool to justify racism in the name of man-made borders.

    Use this worksheet to reflect on migration and how it affects your community. Use your responses to plan ways to aid migrants' safe access to community resources and to honor the cultures and traditions they've brought with them.

Where is my family from? Where are they now? How did they get there?

What countries are my friends and colleagues from? What do I know about their immigration experiences? Or, why do I not have any immigrant friends?

What is an undocumented resident?

What does the term "newest Americans" mean?

What's the difference between refugees and asylum seekers?

Where will I read, watch, or hear first-person stories told by migrants?

How does the Great Northern Migration relate to migration stories of today?

What are the migration experiences of people in my community?

How does race relate to migration experiences in my country?

How does my local, state, and/or federal government monitor undocumented people?

How does my local, state, and/or federal government abuse undocumented people?

How can I support undocumented people in my community?

8

STRENGTH

I define power as the ability to make decisions that affect your own life and the lives of others, the freedom to shape and determine the story of who we are. Power also means having the ability to reward and punish and decide how resources are distributed.

—ALICIA GARZA

The Strength card assures us that we really can get through this. Heart-led and self-controlled, we can push the movement forward in ways that may seem wild compared to the oppressive and marginalizing systems we're used to.

At first glance, this card may appear similar to the Chariot. Strength also relates to power and resolve, but in a more internal fashion. The Chariot points to outer strength while Strength digs into inner power to overcome hurdles. Strength welcomes us to the Major Arcana's second line of interior inquiry after the Chariot's initial outward success and evaluation. Strength recognizes that what they've done so far isn't enough and they must have the fortitude to plow forward. Note that the three-line Major Arcana grid shows the Strength card above the Devil, hinting that we must harness strength to overcome our fears and hang-ups through our personal power.

The Strength card, often representing wild animals, prompts us to perceive our raw selves by noticing our relationships to certain environments. We sometimes may not feel very strong, but maybe we're not in the right spaces for us to safely but bravely exert our human, animalistic, and divine strength. Just as a caged tiger can act out aggressively, we may not react tamely in situations that prevent us from bringing our distinct nature to the table of liberation. We already contain the Strength card's qualities. What does it take for them to emerge in thoughtful and self-controlled ways?

Related to the heart, the Strength archetype shows up with compassion and tolerance. They help others empathize with themselves and other people by illustrating how the interior affects how one presents themselves in the physical realm. This card models gutsy assertion and ardent perseverance through challenges. They also set themselves and others up for success by establishing strategies to deconstruct barriers and prevent burnout.

The Strength archetype can

- Lead with soft power
- Moderate themselves
- Take on stretch projects
- Persuade successfully
- Cultivate positive attitudes
- Show vulnerability
- Serve as a human resources professional, veterinarian, or motivational speaker

Embodied Keywords

Pull out the Strength card from one deck or several. Take a deep breath and pause. Gaze at the imagery. From a liberation perspective, envision yourself in the card's landscape. Be the archetype. Name some keywords that you personally associate with this card. Remember, your definitions are more relevant to your tarot reading than what's in the little white book. Here are a few keywords to help get you started.

> Calmness, tolerance, patience, bravery, compassion, subconscious control, vitality, warmth, self-acceptance, influence, confidence, forgiveness, kindness, generosity, public appearances, willpower, strength in numbers, rewilding, creative urges, transformation, health

✎ **Your keywords:** _____

Strength in Liberation Work

The resilient Strength character is gently powerful in evoking the best out of themselves and their comrades. They don't steamroll; they collaborate. Their power isn't rigid or controlling; it is empathic and guides people to recognize how they can use their assets to demolish racist structures and narratives within themselves and their communities.

To exemplify the Strength card is to know the difference between niceness and kindness. Being nice aims to please and satisfy expectations while being kind is about genuine benevolence. Defending marginalized people often does not look "nice". The kindness shows up in our fight, when we break harmful systems, when we sacrifice privilege for those who are afforded less. Kindness can be rage in evolutionary action. Strength isn't concerned about making everyone happy; they aim to do the right thing. Kindness is a strength.

The Strength card reveals the beast of self-doubt. We don't conquer self-doubt by berating or guilting ourselves for our insecurities. The Strength archetype meets insecurity with compassion and empathy, both for themselves and the people they work with. They remind people of their past successes and that they have what it takes to get past the next obstacle. The work doesn't center on individual confidence or self-assuredness; it orbits the wider world, the issues that are bigger than us. This identity motivates groups to realize that a lack of confidence does not justify giving up. There are things more important than our confidence levels.

Embodying the Strength card looks like reminding people of their motives to sustain fervor. Our ancestors have shown us: the strength of stories creates our shared existence. All our memories exist within mental narratives, like how a breakup is part of a larger story of how you randomly met your sweetie. No history is isolated; everything leads to something else. This character prowls for opportunities to feed and maintain motivation. They're hyperaware of their surroundings, wondering what would be possible if they just kept trying. Will the lion catch their dinner if they move behind a nearby bush? The Strength archetype notices opportunities and imagines stories to plan what's next. They find inspiration and motivation in the story so far, then dare to write the next page. This card is courage exemplified.

Correspondences for Inspiration

Consider exploring sources of inspiration that you connect with the Strength card. To help get you started, here are a few popular associations.

> Lions, serpents, other wild animals, sunflowers, citrus trees, bay leaves, frankincense, tiger's eye, jasper, onyx, cubes, mirrors, roses, the sun, fire, spinal cord, thunderbolts, yellow

✎ **What reminds you of the Strength card? How do these things inspire you to keep going?**

How the Strength Card Can Show Up

There are as many interpretations of tarot as there are people who have ever lived. There is no completely universal card interpretation because there is no completely universal perspective on life. Your and your clients' interpretations are what matter the most during a reading. Of all the possible magical ingredients, we humans are the most powerful in enacting real-world change. However, there are strong collective energies around the themes that appear more frequently when a particular archetype shows up. Here are some of those common motifs.

THE BALANCED STRENGTH ARCHETYPE

- Self-assured
- Heart-led
- Creative
- Community powered
- Caring
- Warm
- Sees people as human beings

✎ **My relationship to the Strength card feels balanced when** _____

- Abuses power
- Forcefully controls
- Ignores their shadows
- Egotistic
- Doesn't believe the world can change
- Overwhelmed
- Closed off

✎ **My relationship to the Strength card feels imbalanced when** _____

Approaching Climate Justice as Racial Justice

After reinventing our now-evolved egos, we plunge into the interior. We face our hearts, and yes, our nightmares. The antidote to our fears exists—where else? In our hearts.

The Strength archetype subdues a beast with genuine care. Climate change is a rapidly growing beast. Earth thrashes to resist human harm, shifting tides and drying tide pools as they stumble out of balance. They're off-kilter because we've pushed them to be. Our planet is hurting. We lament the practical perils of climate change, such as crowded landfills, displaced migrants, xenophobia, limited resources, and war. What if we peered into the Earth's spirit to reveal more about this climate beast?

The planet has been hurt, misunderstood, mistreated, and taken for granted.
Not a beast, just hurt.
In return, they snarl back.
Not a beast, just hurt.
They bark, howl, and roar over and through riptides.
Not a beast, just hurt.

We respond to our loved ones' pain not with resistance or backlash, but with love.

We fight our beasts with love. This is soft power, this is care. This is an intimate passion with multivarious forms. Climate justice is love justice is racial justice is strength justice.

When holding the Strength card, you might channel Saturn in Leo—two archetypes often affiliated with Strength through key eight. Saturn's task-mindedness feels heavy. The work is dark, tedious, and long-fought. It is tempting (and easier) to stay home. But Leo radiates inward and lightens Saturn's spirit by reminding it of what's important and why. Here, courage sparks.

Consider this celestial relationship when you think about your actions against unprecedented climate change, a severe beast. Think about this; then look around. Hear the birds singing. Feel the grass beneath your feet. Smell the pine needles. Watch the trees sway with the wind. Conjure awe for all the necessities and pleasures nature provides. All around, we have reasons to resist climate violence. Love for the planet is a soft power that can fill the courage tanks that fuel our racial justice work.

Remember how far soft, loving power can go and the many benevolent forms it can take.

Wherever you are in the world, it is the underserved—the poor, the overlooked, the vulnerable—who most acutely feel the impact of climate change. As many of these people are Black and Brown, there are plenty of links—obvious and covert—between climate abuse and racial abuse. Residential segregation, cities' uneven political representation, limited economic opportunities—these things are just a few oppressive systems that escalate marginalized people's direct exposure to climate crises.

Let's shift our gaze specifically at the United States.

Disproportionate numbers of Black people live in areas with toxic waste that leads to racially discrepant health outcomes across the nation: heart problems, high blood pressure, cancer, asthma, infections. A 2018 report from the Environmental Protection Agency indicated that race influences exposure to pollutants significantly even more than poverty.

People of color often suffer first, and often the worst. For instance, many companies produce toxic waste that seeps into the water of low-income communities. And sometimes they purposely pick predominately Black locations. We breathe in air quality that is damaged. We have more stillbirths. We strain existing health conditions, causing acute and lifelong illnesses. We witness disparities in disaster recovery aid. We see death, time and time again.

Do you know that over half the people who died during Hurricane Katrina were Black? Or that 80 percent of the destroyed homes were Black-owned? These are American examples, but anti-Blackness exists around the world and it's not difficult to find more instances of people of color on the front lines of climate emergencies.

Climate justice is love justice is racial justice is strength justice—
—harness your heart.

Plenty of climate activist groups, notably the predominately white ones, do not prioritize their work with racial justice in mind. Instead, they may focus on reusable bags or driving electric cars.

The fight goes beyond our compost piles.

Individually, it is a loving offering to Earth when we live more sustainably. At the same time, just 100 companies are responsible for 71 percent of the global greenhouse gas emissions since 1998. As teenage climate activist Alexandria Villaseñor stated, "The exploitation of Black people is the greatest extractive system of production of all time, and in order to heal the planet, we must have Black and Indigenous liberation." Again, people of color around the world typically suffer the first and the most from climate emergencies. Yet the connection between climate justice and racial justice has only recently caught on in collective discourses.

The catching on isn't catching up fast enough, and we're on our way to a global average temperature rise of 4°C by the end of the century.

There's no quick fix when the beast's complexity runs deep. Yet the systems—its defenses—must fall. We do this for all we love in this earthly experience. Climate justice work is a courageous effort of love. We demonstrate love by noticing what we fund when we spend our money at different businesses. Like the Lovers said, money is power in capitalist regimes.

Journal where you spend your money for a week. Then find climate scorecards on those businesses. Is your money helping desolate a life-sustaining river or funding a conscious reforestation project?

Again, there's no quick fix. It's problematic that I am typing this from my MacBook. But I'm starting to think about my relationships with the planet, my loved ones, and my money more intentionally, thoughtfully, and generatively. We tend to our beasts with love, however love manifests. We must practice the inconvenience of saying goodbye the more we devote ourselves to the future. Reroute money, time, and attention toward organizations that commit to climate and racial justice and eliminate policies that marginalize or otherwise harm people of color. Changing habits requires soft power with ourselves. A harsh, forced push encourages resistance; self-forgiveness and bravery ease the transition to our next level of dedication.

It takes loving power and courage to align our actions and resources with our values, even more when it is inconvenient or unconventional.

SUGGESTED EXERCISES

1. Check out the "Climate Change in the African American Community" fact sheet by Moms Clean Air Force and adopt at least one practice from the "What You Can Do About Climate Change" section.

2. Research Cancer Alley and reflect upon your learnings.

3. Read "Focusing on How Individuals Can Stop Climate Change Is Very Convenient for Corporations" on Fast Company. Then divest from at least one major corporate offender.

4. Read "Are Crystals the New Blood Diamonds?" by Eva Wiseman or "Dark Crystals: The Brutal Reality Behind a Booming Wellness Craze" by Tess McClure, both from the *Guardian*. List the ethical implications of how you acquire and use crystals.

5. Revisit the tools that you use in your spiritual practice, such as white sage, and research whether it is ethical for you to use them. Reflect on the harm you are potentially perpetuating, and act on what you discover.

6. Perform a tangible spell for the planet.

Identifying as the Strength Archetype

How do you already embody Strength? Use this list of words commonly associated with this card to identify the qualities that you do and don't want to work with as you help create a radically more equitable world.

- Circle the qualities you already embody and can leverage as a superpower.
- Draw a heart around the qualities you want to embody more deeply or frequently.
- Draw a square around the qualities you want to transmute or avoid.

Knows their potential impact	Demanding	Aware of their instincts	Lacks self-discipline	Creative
Courageous	Frantic	Deep listener	Positive	Recognizes others' strengths
Daring	Patient	Encouraging	Confident	Kind
Unsure	Actions don't match goals	Heart-led	Powerful	Transformative

Affirmations for Embodying the Strength Card

When you lean into your inner strength, you might choose an affirmation to motivate you when the work is difficult. Affirmations can strengthen commitment by supporting your confidence in achieving personal and community goals. They can also help combat fear, anxiety, self-doubt, and loss of motivation, which are common feelings that come up in social justice work. You can chant them, write them down, meditate on them, add them to your phone background, or otherwise work with them consistently to keep focused on your objectives. Here are some examples.

"I show up as my whole self."

"I'm braver than I was yesterday."

"I am at once rageful and calm."

"I belong here."

"I'm stronger than my impulses."

✎ Often, the most powerful affirmations are the ones we create for ourselves. Take some time to jot down your personal affirmations.

Magical Practices to Conjure the Strength Card

Disprove self-doubt by listing times when you have been strong. Create more equitable access to local exercise and wellness facilities. Make sure you are physically prepared before attending a protest. Find your unique place in your movement. Ask yourself who gets to be vulnerable in your society and why. Reclaim your inherent wildness. Be tender. Show up more visibly. Work with partners to increase outcomes. Help underserved people pursue passions. Embody the Queen of Wands. Notice your instincts. Attend to the power dynamics in your organization.

Becoming the Strength Archetype

Meditate on your relationship with the Strength card and use what you know to plan real-world action. By responding to these prompts, you are committing to doing the work—period.

SET A PERSONAL, RELATIONAL, OR COLLECTIVE INTENTION

✎ Name an objective that your work will center around.

✎ Plan specific actions for this objective that you will take as you embody Strength.

✎ This [day/week/month/event], I will embody Strength in my liberation work by ___

✎ This work is important because _____

✎ The affirmation I will repeat is _____

REFLECT ON YOUR EXPERIENCE

✎ Evolution is iterative and often nonlinear. As we pursue our goals, we must regularly evaluate our actions, mistakes, and learnings to inform the next cycles of change. Review your experience and identify what you can take with you as you move through your antiracism work.

- Successes
- Setbacks
- Frustrations
- Questions
- Other reflections
- Next steps

BUILDING A TOOLKIT

Defend the Climate

The Strength card relates to our wild, natural selves. We are nature; there is no separation. We harm nature, and thus ourselves, by forcing climate change. Again, people of color often suffer the most.

You might not save the world, but you can always start somewhere. Answer the following prompts and use your responses to determine several ways that you will defend the planet through local change.

What is the environmental justice movement?

How does the environmental justice movement show up in your household?

How does the environmental justice movement show up in your local community?

How does the environmental justice movement show up in your organization?

What is your local government doing to combat climate change?

What are some environmental justice groups in your area?

How does the climate crisis impact the lives of the global majority?

How does the climate crisis impact the lives of your neighbors?

What are some personal motivations behind your climate activism?

9

THE HERMIT

They ask me to remember
but they want me to remember
their memories
and I keep on remembering mine.
—LUCILLE CLIFTON

The Hermit deepens their intimacy with themselves to deepen their intimacy with the world. Parallel to the Sun in Virgo, they commit to deliberate thought processes, devoted practice, and keen discrimination on their path toward enlightenment. The Hermit goes within, but they always come back.

Introspection is the Hermit's game. After completing the assignments of keys one to eight, they retreat and get quiet enough to palpably hear their inner selves. This self-inquiry is mysterious, but the Hermit is willing to witness anything they may discover. They might even hope to be surprised. They withdraw from society to become more impartial in their self-reflection. Card nine reviews their past efforts and their impact to determine the necessary mindset for returning to their community. They revisit the focus of their devotion in the context of current events and reaffirm their mission. This reflection leads to personal transformation, which ripples into collective change after the Hermit returns to civilization a changed person. Personal and cultural evolution transforms their work. This work is often discreet; sometimes it's easier to change when we're alone.

The Hermit retreats, but they don't indulge in a room full of fancy tools and trinkets. This archetype perceives their knowledge and intuition as lanterns guiding their growth. They dispose of the unnecessary to reinforce and purify their connection to their divine purpose—liberation. A clearer vision enables the

Hermit to help their community evolve ideas and beliefs about what the future could look like.

This card is sometimes referred to as "the crone." In the maiden, mother, and crone life sequence, the crone is the most proximal to death and the universe's enigmas. The Hermit doesn't retreat to escape the world; they do it to get closer to the mysterious divine within. They return to the world more enlightened, and thus with more to share of their wisdom thoughtfully informed by experience and diverse sources.

The Hermit can

- Evaluate their objectives regularly
- Work on independent projects
- Practice compassionate detachment
- Help others see their inner light
- Be a keen observer
- Eschew materialism
- Serve as a meditation guide, scientist, mentor, or editor

Embodied Keywords

Pull out the Hermit card from one deck or several. Take a deep breath and pause. Gaze at the imagery. From a liberation perspective, envision yourself in the card's landscape. Be the archetype. Name some keywords that you personally associate with this card. Remember, your definitions are more relevant to your tarot reading than what's in the little white book. Here are a few keywords to help get you started.

Integrity, introspection, boundaries, wisdom, soul-searching, evaluation, analytical processes, giving space, maturity, revealing the root, review, mystery, divinity, withdrawal, solitude, prudence, guidance, seeking truth, sharing insights, pilgrimage, depth, decommodification, age, contentment with oneself

 Your keywords: _____

The Hermit in Liberation Work

The Hermit may seem passive, but their internal work directly affects their movement's progress. Their reclusion is active and purposeful. To get a better sense of how they can accelerate social justice efforts, they get a better sense of themselves. They critically and honestly gaze deep within themselves, eliciting information about how they have and haven't been effective, recent deviations from values and beliefs, how their inner light shows up in their work, and how their learnings equip them to mentor others. In returning to the world, they transform their reflections into actions for themselves and their movements.

The Hermit is attentive, sometimes taking notes during meetings or measuring impact. They don't just look; they notice. They note connections between actions, people, and themes and bring them to team discussions about next steps. They're simultaneously retrospective and forward-thinking.

This archetype honors quiet. They create spaces for silence and rest for marginalized communities. They amplify ways that introverted people can participate in causes. They remind their peers to think before they act. They lead free meditation classes. The Hermit views peace as an avenue for self-development, which intertwines with societal development.

The Hermit reflects, then determines what's necessary and unnecessary. They take stock of their team's assets, such as equipment and money, then identify where their energy may be leaking. The Hermit actively participates in conversations about asset management and opportunities for financial reprioritization. They don't hesitate to relinquish outdated tools and expired narratives when it's time to let them go.

Correspondences for Inspiration

Consider exploring sources of inspiration that you associate with the Hermit. To help get you started, here are a few popular ones.

> Owls, cats, bears, squirrels, beech, chestnut, mimosa trees, petrified wood, aster, sandalwood, narcissus, juniper, myrrh, carnelian, mercury, aluminum, peridot, zircon, bloodstone, mountains, lights

✎ What reminds you of the Hermit? How do these things inspire you to keep going?

How the Hermit Can Show Up

There are as many interpretations of tarot as there are people who have ever lived. There is no completely universal card interpretation because there is no completely universal perspective on life. Your and your clients' interpretations are what matter the most during a reading. Of all the possible magical ingredients, we humans are the most powerful in enacting real-world change. However, there are strong collective energies around the themes that appear more frequently when a particular archetype shows up. Here are some of those common motifs.

THE BALANCED HERMIT

- Surrenders to mystery
- Confronts their mistakes
- Is comfortable being alone
- Reflects regularly
- Acts as a lighthouse for others
- Remains flexible
- Practices grounding

My relationship to the Hermit feels balanced when _____

THE IMBALANCED HERMIT

- Isolates themselves excessively
- Superficial
- Self-righteous
- Resists constructive criticism
- Claims others' stories as their own
- Feels disconnected or exiled
- Materialistic

My relationship to the Hermit feels imbalanced when _____

Turning the Lantern toward Emotional Labor

Turning inward commences the process of understanding what we've learned thus far and how we can leverage that information for purposeful change. Our revelations are a light that we can turn and shine on others.

The Rider-Waite-Smith deck depicts the Hermit by themselves, contemplating and holding a lantern. The Hermit is in a place that looks far different from the dominant experience. This place may seem quite remote. It could also be for the Hermit—or it could be rather familiar. Who knows?

We might not know the catalyst for this pilgrimage. We often picture the Hermit as someone who willingly sets out on this spiritual venture and learns profound and sometimes beautiful things. But what if we reenvisioned them as a visitor to a strange new place without a choice? What if we imagined them as bigger than one person, but as a people or the soul of generational wisdom or trauma? What if the Hermit didn't want to go on this exhausting journey, but they had to? What if we asked: How long has the Hermit—this soul—been here? How many lives has the Hermit lived?

They carry a lantern to shine on the community to which they must return. The lantern—the information, the lessons, the insight—illuminates for others what the Hermit gathered upon the mountaintop. Notice that the Hermit isn't coerced or in chains—the choice to share light is what it is: a choice.

In myriad arenas, white people expect BIPOC to illuminate them with knowledge about marginalized experiences. Their requests may be unintentional, but their questions, prompts, and unsolicited musings often indicate expectations for people to engage, even if only by listening to tales of white guilt. The expectation is free emotional labor.

The term "emotional labor" came into widespread use after sociologist Arlie Hochschild described it in *The Managed Heart* as having to "induce or suppress feeling in order to sustain the outward countenance that produces the proper state of mind in others." This lens can describe much of what patriarchal culture demands of women in general, but emotional labor can also bear heavy implications when thoughtlessly solicited from racially oppressed groups, particularly individuals at multiple intersections.

Focusing on the Black American experience, emotional labor takes many forms in many environments. Examples include being

- Prompted to explain one's identity
- Pressured to shrug off microaggressions
- Prompted to share triggering information that is easily searchable on Google
- Forced into hypervisibility
- Urged to subdue justifiable rage
- Expected to protect white comfort and safety at the loss of one's own comfort and safety
- Put in a position to defend one's intelligence
- Challenged to prove the validity of one's racialized experience
- Treated as the token person for conversations about Blackness
- Cloaked in monolithic beliefs about Blackness instead of being seen as an individual
- Asked to serve as an example of Blackness, such as being called on in the classroom more often during Black History Month

The Work is the Work, and it doesn't mean starting uninvited conversations with someone you barely know about how awful a white supremacist rally was or about police brutality. The Work is considering what you will say to and ask from someone before you speak. The Work is being well-meaning and well-doing. The Work offers many ways to be present for Black liberation without defaulting to the assumption that Black people will freely siphon precious emotional energy to explain things for you. Think about what you expect before you ask.

Some white people respond to Black emotional labor fatigue by saying things like, "Why should you even respond at all?" and "Preserve yourself and don't take on more than you can handle." Yet being Black in this world is more than a lot of us can handle. Black people are often highly aware of the potential social consequences to declining white people's queries, so we sometimes feel compelled to speak up.

Black people are sentient, complex human beings who aren't here to educate you. They are not a perpetually renewable learning resource.

The Work means taking on some of the burden, such as the weight of research, catching up, waiting for answers, locating answers, examples, and stories. The Work is frequently inconvenient. Still, chances are that there is a book, video, or article on the subject you're about to ask someone to explain to you.

There's no need to automatically assume the right to drain Black energy. Some people of color teach from experience when they have capacity to share painful stories of trauma. Plenty of such material is free to access online.

Use your privilege to shine your lantern onto the world by finding, accessing, and using resources to delegitimize oppressive forces.

Yes, shine your light onto systemic oppression. The world needs it.

SUGGESTED EXERCISES

1. Watch or listen to Monica Johnson's "The Emotional Cost of Being a Black Woman in America" (16 min).

2. Read "How to Compensate Black Women and Femmes on Social Media for Their Emotional Labor" by Threads of Solidarity.

3. Consider budgeting compensation to Black teachers who influence and motivate your work. If you don't, ask what you can do to fit it in your budget.

4. Write a list of thoughts or times when you have played the devil's advocate in conversations about race; then reflect on your thought processes and why it was inappropriate.

5. Find events to connect with less privileged people in real time—not for the purpose of requesting emotional labor, but for learning about their life without demanding information.

Identifying as the Hermit

How do you already embody the Hermit? Use this list of words commonly associated with this card to identify the qualities that you do and don't want to work with as you help create a radically more equitable world.

- ■ Circle the qualities you already embody and can leverage as a superpower.
- ■ Draw a heart around the qualities you want to embody more deeply or frequently.
- ■ Draw a square around the qualities you want to transmute or avoid.

Wise	Resourceful	Superficial	Attentive	Misanthrope
Inflexible beliefs	Listens to inner guidance	Resists feedback	Acts without thinking	Grounds energy
Devoted	Learns from elders	Makes alone time	Respects sacredness	Shares knowledge
Lonely	Ignores inner flame	Distracted	Inspiring	Doesn't keep in touch

Affirmations for Embodying the Hermit

When you practice the Hermit's intentional solitude, you might choose an affirmation to motivate you when the work is difficult. Affirmations can strengthen commitment by supporting your confidence in achieving personal and community goals. They can also help combat fear, anxiety, self-doubt, and loss of motivation, which are common feelings that come up in social justice work. You can chant them, write them down, meditate on them, add them to your phone background, or otherwise work with them consistently to keep focused on your objectives. Here are some examples.

"I act with integrity and humility."

"I am already prepared to meet my interior."

"I surrender to the mystery and welcome its wisdom."

"My wisdom becomes meaningful when I share it."

"I will never dim my light."

✎ Often, the most powerful affirmations are the ones we create for ourselves. Take some time to jot down your personal affirmations.

Magical Practices to Conjure the Hermit

Directly interact with marginalized groups. Create quiet safe spaces for your community. Cut cords with what doesn't support your cause. Fund a camp or another retreat for underserved children. Design an informational and accessible zine. Encourage others' commitment. Build stages where people can share insights. Donate relaxation devices to a local organization. Become a mentor. Separate your core identity from your past mistakes. Embody your personal divinity during interactions. Lighten burdens. Lead team retrospectives. Make incremental changes. Steer new initiatives based on practical wisdom.

Becoming the Hermit

Meditate on your relationship with the Hermit and use what you know to plan real-world action. By responding to these prompts, you are committing to doing the work—period.

SET A PERSONAL, RELATIONAL, OR COLLECTIVE INTENTION

✎ Name an objective that your work will center around.

✎ Plan specific actions for this objective that you will take as you embody the Hermit.

✎ This [day/week/month/event], I will embody the Hermit in my liberation work by

✎ This work is important because _____

✎ The affirmation I will repeat is _____

REFLECT ON YOUR EXPERIENCE

✎ Evolution is iterative and often nonlinear. As we pursue our goals, we must regularly evaluate our actions, mistakes, and learnings to inform the next cycles of change. Review your experience and identify what you can take with you as you move through your antiracism work.

- Successes
- Setbacks
- Frustrations
- Questions
- Other reflections
- Next steps

Protect Unhoused People

In search of enlightenment, the Hermit retreats to a safe space. This place must feel secure. Exposure to outside elements may hinder the pursuit of self-actualization. The importance of protection is widely apparent in our society, manifesting in forms such as houselessness. Learn the realities of your community's unhoused people and plan ways that you will help protect them.

Describe your own or a loved one's experience of houselessness.

What are the racial statistics on houselessness in your city?

How does race intersect with houselessness?

What are ten ways that you will support your community's unhoused people in the next six months?

10

THE WHEEL OF FORTUNE

Why can so many of us effortlessly engage in nuanced discussion of white supremacist capitalist cis hetero patriarchal imperialism and yet be completely incapable of identifying ableism?

—TALILA A. LEWIS

The Wheel of Fortune is reminiscent of the universe's unpredictability. Masses of news cycles prove this every day. Routinely, something outside of our control happens and changes our collective destiny. The Wheel of Fortune boldly embodies the reality that everything changes. No river is the same twice. Good situations sour and bad situations improve—and there exist endless possibilities within and beyond that spectrum. Uninterruptible, the wheel of time rotates while we try to prepare for its upcoming movements. How we interact with the wheel informs our resolve during unpredictable events. If we expect change, our reactions are softer than when we resist it.

The Wheel stays ready. Luck is where preparation and opportunity meet.

This archetype is highly aware of what's unfolding and the cards that they have been dealt. This is a card of movement, demanding that we don't get too comfortable when the going is good or feel too defeated when things don't operate smoothly. Assured that the future is always on its way, the Wheel of Fortune respects that the only constant is change. They highlight their life cycles, relationships, and environments and exemplify flexibility when deciding how to go with the flow. They don't expect to reach their goals in a perpetually changing world using fixed perspectives about how things "should" be. They pursue their goals while clearing space for unexpected opportunities and reasons to change directions or conditions.

The Wheel of Fortune doesn't attempt to control other people. Appearing after the Hermit, this archetype has a solid sense of self and the wisdom to discern what's their responsibility and what's not, especially when the latter is out of their hands. Rather, they focus their energy on taking advantage of new opportunities as soon as they arise because experience has proven that certain opportunities may never return. Their work is effective because they remain present. When distracted, they look past unforeseen chances to evolve with flow.

The Wheel of Fortune can

- Seize the moment
- Honor natural cycles
- Be real about their circumstances
- Exhibit exemplary patience
- Handle major changes calmly and flexibly
- Work in multiple timelines
- Serve as a farmer, public speaker, investor, or freelancer

Embodied Keywords

Pull out the Wheel of Fortune card from one deck or several. Take a deep breath and pause. Gaze at the imagery. From a liberation perspective, envision yourself in the card's landscape. Be the archetype. Name some keywords that you personally associate with this card. Remember, your definitions are more relevant to your tarot reading than what's in the little white book. Here are a few keywords to help get you started.

> Fate, cycles, turning points, mutability, karma, faith, optimism, turning tides, life's mysteries, pivots, saving for rainy days, surprise opportunities, self-accountability, risk evaluation, hope, trust, balance, endings as beginnings, synchronicities, presence, independence, free will, reset buttons, universal laws, timing, flexibility, acceptance

Your keywords: _____

The Wheel of Fortune in Liberation Work

The Wheel of Fortune lives in the moment, finding synchronicities and opportunities that can advance their cause. They read weekly bulletins, keep up with local news, write newsletters, look out for grants, and maintain connections with other revolutionary individuals and groups. They absolutely believe that their goals are possible and that opportunities to promote progress can appear at any given moment.

For the wheel of the universe to continue turning, this radical archetype must compromise at times. They're artists of bargaining without folding. Their goals are evergreen, but they can't hoard strategies when the world revolves non-stop; they can't take everything with them. The Wheel of Fortune altruistically shakes up "the way things were" for the greater good of their communities. They mediate, prioritize, and ensure consistent, sustainable momentum. Time eternally advances into the unknown and the wheel is responsible for their ability to endure temporal cycles.

The Wheel is expansive when they determine what is within their domain. The contrast of what's outside of one's control outlines what's actually in their control. They don't fixate on personal ideas of what the world to come should look like because they know that tomorrow could look *even better*. Future realities may not fully reflect modern expectations; thus the Wheel wears a wide lens of possibility. The Wheel of Fortune is realistic but makes space for unforeseen opportunities because the only thing promised to change is time.

Correspondences for Inspiration

Consider exploring sources of inspiration that you associate with the Wheel of Fortune. To help get you started, here are a few popular correspondences.

> Mars conjunct Jupiter, whales, spiders, deer, hens, dolphins, domestic animals, dandelion, elm, beech, clove, fruit trees, leeks, figs, pineapples, rhubarb, mastic, anise, elm, saffron, balm of Gilead, odiferous fruits, amethyst, lapis lazuli, marble, tin, gold, silver, zinc, clocks, seasons

 What reminds you of the Wheel of Fortune? How do they inspire you to keep going?

How the Wheel of Fortune Can Show Up

There are as many interpretations of tarot as there are people who have ever lived. There is no completely universal card interpretation because there is no completely universal perspective on life. Your and your clients' interpretations are what matter the most during a reading. Of all the possible magical ingredients, we humans are the most powerful in enacting real-world change. However, there are strong collective energies around the themes that appear more frequently when a particular archetype shows up. Here are some of those common motifs.

THE BALANCED WHEEL OF FORTUNE

- Remains connected to their central mission
- Learns quickly from mistakes
- Pivots when necessary
- Considers adversity temporary
- Displays optimism
- Negotiates fairly
- Turns lemons into lemonade

✎ My relationship to the Wheel of Fortune feels balanced when _____

THE IMBALANCED WHEEL OF FORTUNE

- Controls excessively
- Refuses to switch gears
- Battles indecision
- Gives up easily
- Ignores signs
- Expects instant results
- Feels powerless

✎ My relationship to the Wheel of Fortune feels imbalanced when _____

Intersecting Race and Disability Justice

The Wheel of Fortune knows all control and no control at the same time. They find their anchor in their center.

The many-faceted Wheel asks us to reflect upon universal themes, such as fate and cyclicity. Let's turn our gaze toward a potent symbol of this archetype: the grasp.

To grasp ourselves can be to own ourselves. When we do this lovingly, we commit to knowing what and who we are. Our racial justice work disrupts others' harmful, monolithic stereotypes and assumptions about marginalized people. In fairness, we should also disrupt our own preconceptions.

We must grasp the intersectionality of our work.

The Wheel is a spherical reminder to pull ourselves back into gravitational alignment with our values. Sometimes we can't see how we are living our values until we adopt the long view. Many of our perceptions only become overtly visible when we take a step back for a less partial perspective.

Step back and contemplate whether your work is currently healthy, purposeful, inclusive, and evolving.

Key ten, reduced to the number 1 after adding 1 + 0, appears after the Hermit—reiterating that we are individual people, self-owning and self-responsible. Our need to hold our own center is just as important as it is for others. Our work does not work when we assume that our sense of "normal" is the same for others.

What is normal when there is room for everybody? We must shift, involve, adapt, and evolve. No one's free until we're all free.

Minding the intersections between the racial justice and disability justice movements is key to expanding and redefining access in our societies. Still, the subject of disability can be treated as a fringe topic in racial justice efforts even though it's integral to broadening our potential for success.

Ableism, deeply and intentionally embedded in our lives' frameworks, is discrimination against people based on dominant expectations of "normal ability." People consciously and unconsciously use these expectations to ignore, disregard, and subjugate disabled people, especially those without jobs and thus less capital.

The threads of racism and ableism have been woven together throughout history to uphold physically and mentally harmful stigmas and justify racial oppression.

Consider the nineteenth-century scientific concept of *drapetomania*, a word to describe the perceived mental illness of enslaved Black people who sought to flee captivity. The white-dominant medical field deemed former slaves on the run to be mentally ill. Doctors and scientists were convinced that these people were mentally incompetent and needed treatment (for example, lashings) to return to desired "normal" behavior.

As the wheel turns, we stretch and contain conceptual boundaries—for better or worse. For instance, disability, self- and other-defined, weighs heavy at the intersection of Blackness and ability. Here is a brief list of significant examples:

Sixty to eighty percent of people murdered by police are disabled people. Ableism is well integrated into the school-to-prison pipeline, as children with disabilities are pushed into the legal system five to six times more often than children without identified disabilities. Note that around 13 percent of the U.S. population is Black, yet so is over 34 percent of the entire country's incarcerated population.

Access to resources is especially limited for disabled Black people, as people with disabilities are more likely to be poor. Know that poverty is both a cause and consequence of disability.

Courts often refuse to accommodate people with disabilities, leading to an array of avoidable problems. For example, a deaf man who used Ethiopian Sign Language was denied an interpreter for court and jail, leaving him to spend six weeks in jail for a crime he didn't commit.

Black people with disabilities are vulnerable to many levels of structural oppression, and ableism often criminalizes the presence of qualities that deviate from stringent societal norms. If you haven't incorporated disability justice into your racial equity work, now may be a good time to start.

The pathologization of Black people is partially responsible for establishing and maintaining societal barriers. Structurally oppressive institutions rarely discuss how their actions create a landscape where disability is increasingly unavoidable. Ableism can beget racism and racism can beget ableism. Racial justice and disability justice groups must witness each other's experiences. Their experiences of oppression may vary, but they ultimately intersect in the overall resistance against the tyranny of white, able-bodied dominance.

We must grasp that disabled bodies are not pathology, but beings deserving of global liberation.

The wheel, it turns. And we can grasp it too.

SUGGESTED EXERCISES

1. If you are in a coven or another group, audit your expectations and practices for inclusivity.

2. Follow the work of Black disabled organizers, such as Vilissa Thompson and Walela Nehanda, who do critical work in the field of disability and racial justice.

3. Read and meditate upon Sins Invalid's "10 Principles of Disability Justice."

4. Review the resources in "Black Disabled Woman Syllabus: A Compilation."

5. Watch or listen to Keri Gray speak in "Disability Is Intersectional" (captioned, 1 minute).

6. Never act like you are the spokesperson for all people with your disability.

Identifying as the Wheel of Fortune

How do you already embody the Wheel of Fortune? Use this list of words commonly associated with this card to identify the qualities that you do and don't want to work with as you help create a radically more equitable world.

- Circle the qualities you already embody and can leverage as a superpower.

- Draw a heart around the qualities you want to embody more deeply or frequently.

- Draw a square around the qualities you want to transmute or avoid.

Energized by change	Disagreeable	Unpredictable	Aware of opportunities	Dynamic
Aligned to their mission	Evasive	Holds their center	Aloof	Stays prepared
Pessimistic	Single-minded	Puts all eggs in one basket	Noncommittal	Adaptable
Short-term vision	Hopeful	Inspires momentum	Trusting	Controls tightly

Affirmations for Embodying the Wheel of Fortune

When you ride along the Wheel of Fortune's revolutions, you might choose an affirmation to motivate you when the work is difficult. Affirmations can strengthen commitment by supporting your confidence in achieving personal and community goals. They can also help combat fear, anxiety, self-doubt, and loss of motivation, which are common feelings that come up in social justice work. You can chant them, write them down, meditate on them, add them to your phone background, or otherwise work with them consistently to keep focused on your objectives. Here are some examples.

"I hold my center wherever I flow."

"I stay ready."

"What I do today shows up tomorrow."

"Every day I romance my center of stability."

"I'm here for the long haul."

Often, the most powerful affirmations are the ones we create for ourselves. Take some time to jot down your personal affirmations.

Magical Practices to Conjure the Wheel of Fortune

Embed mutual aid into your budget. Release and share control. Stay alert for unexpected ways your organization can get more involved in the community. Make a toolkit for recuperating morale. Act on cycles of injustice. Watch for confirmation bias. Mediate when conflict arises. Write a personal definition of free will. Incorporate time magic into your social justice work. Unstuck people. Accept impermanence. Change your daily routine. Review your commitments. Make sure your everyday choices align with a more ideal future. Know that your actions have consequences.

Becoming the Wheel of Fortune

Meditate on your relationship with the Wheel of Fortune, and use what you know to plan real-world action. By responding to these prompts, you are committing to doing the work—period.

SET A PERSONAL, RELATIONAL, OR COLLECTIVE INTENTION

- Name an objective that your work will center around.

- Plan specific actions for this objective that you will take as you embody the Wheel of Fortune.

- This [day/week/month/event], I will embody the Wheel of Fortune in my liberation work by _____

- This work is important because _____

- The affirmation I will repeat is _____

REFLECT ON YOUR EXPERIENCE

- Evolution is iterative and often nonlinear. As we pursue our goals, we must regularly evaluate our actions, mistakes, and learnings to inform the next cycles of change.

Review your experience and identify what you can take with you as you move through your antiracism work.

- Successes

- Setbacks

- Frustrations

- Questions

- Other reflections

- Next steps

BUILDING A TOOLKIT

Expand Health Care Access

The Wheel of Fortune invokes each of us to hold our center as the world turns, to grasp onto something stable while human unpredictability reveals itself. This is grounding. Grounding work often involves our physical body, our instrument to connect with the Earth, from the soles of our feet to the planet's fiery core. When we attune to our bodies, we may discover health needs.

Health care systems around the globe deny equitable access to quality health care. Most of the people affected are nonwhite. We can't heal everyone, but we can influence our communities' medical systems to expand accessible healing opportunities.

Take a few minutes to explore the history and current state of health care; then strategize how you will help decolonize the medical industry.

What is medical racism? Define it.

List five real-world examples of medical racism.

What are some facts about the history of health insurance in your community?

What are the negative implications of tying health insurance to employment?

What health policies has your city enacted? How do they affect you and your neighbors?

Name some racial health disparities in your city, province, and country.
Consider issues like heart disease, maternal health, mental health, and cancer.

What's the real history of medical experimentation on nonwhite bodies?

How does white supremacy affect perceptions of mental illness?

How does the legal system criminalize mental illness?

What are your town's local free or sliding scale mental health resources?

How does the legal system criminalize disability?

How does your social justice work prioritize disability justice?

How can you make meetings, protests, or other events more accessible?

How can you help expand BIPOC access to safe medical care?

11

JUSTICE

A crown, if it hurts us, is not worth wearing.

—PEARL BAILEY

Right in the middle of the Major Arcana's second row sits Justice. Here is a stable position for fairly evaluating our outer and inner growth before proceeding toward the line of the collective superconscious. Justice points to the middle way. Stationed above the Moon, Justice says that we become more whole when we align with and act in truth. This archetype contemplates the causes and their effects. For every choice we make, there are options we rejected. Justice makes mindful sacrifices and shepherds people through decision-making processes.

Justice notices where their energy goes and checks for any spots of energetic leakage. Often depicted with weight scales, this character ensures balance between what they give and what they receive or achieve. Excessive work for insufficient results is time wasted. Exorbitant results from minimal work suggests they have more to offer.

This card advocates for fairness, but they know that concepts of "fairness" are complicated. The more they experience the world and interact with different people, the more they graduate from black-and-white thinking into spacious gray areas. Justice relates the micro to the macro. Our individual lives constitute the micro, which shapes the collective, the macro. As such, Justice wields their sword of discrimination wisely, aware that there is no singular path toward liberation. What works here might not work there. What fills one's cup might drain another's. Multiple truths can be true at once. Justice meticulously considers how their actions impact their communities and determines, with crystal clear intention, future actions through highly contextual lenses of truth and balance.

Many tarot resources describe Justice as it pertains to the external world, but this archetype also affects our personal lives. Justice recognizes when it's time to go hard and when it's time to rest. Inspired by the Wheel of Fortune's lessons, Justice cultivates a balanced center that they can hold on to as conditions go in and out of balance. Mission, integrity, and honesty configure Justice's steadfast core.

The Justice archetype can

- Read between the lines
- Sacrifice personal gain for what's fair
- Admit their biases
- Mediate effectively
- Own up to their mistakes
- Model how to live in one's truth
- Serve as a legal advocate, parent, budget manager, or investigator

Embodied Keywords

Pull out the Justice card from one deck or several. Take a deep breath and pause. Gaze at the imagery. From a liberation perspective, envision yourself in the card's landscape. Be the archetype. Name some keywords that you personally associate with this card. Remember, your definitions are more relevant to your tarot reading than what's in the little white book. Here are a few keywords to help get you started.

> Alignment, decision-making, truth, domino effects, guidelines, accountability, logic, benefit of the doubt, ethics, order, objectivity, legal affairs, contracts, formalization, balance, integrity, remediation, options, harmony, tests, conviction, cultural and situational awareness, education, cord-cutting, conflict resolution, sacrifice

Your keywords: _____

Justice in Liberation Work

Key eleven's digits add together to make two, connecting Justice to the High Priestess (key two). This pairing alludes to how we balance intuition with objectivity and fair judgment in the pursuit of justice. Justice calmly and curiously encounters liminal spaces and pairs their gut with the facts to make choices that ultimately lead to a more equitable society. Justice says that there is no single path that fits for everybody in every place and time. Many roads lead to collective freedom. They consult assemblies to institute policies based on modern realities, not what we wish our current world would be. Justice recognizes that all decisions are tinted by the people who make them, so they check in with their inner self to discover and address biases that masquerade as intuition.

Justice initiates and sustains accessibility efforts because they seek fairness. They are aware that disabilities are common, acknowledge invisible disabilities, respect diverse activist participation, honor intersections, and center community care. They make it safe for peers to voice accessibility requests prior to events. They notice who dominates conversations and who elevates lesser-known voices. Accessibility determines their venue choices. They supply online components to in-person events, when possible.

Justice holds people—themselves, their loved ones, their organizations, and public servants—accountable. The natural law of cause and effect indicates that there are always consequences, that our actions reverberate. Yet legal systems around the world enforce sentences that aren't commensurate with related crimes. The Justice card holds despots, big business, the police, and other harmful entities to account. They also do this internally. They admit how they've oppressed others, and remedy the harm. As much as possible, their remedies' impact matches the depth of the offense. Justice symbolizes the necessary integrity to genuinely sacrifice comfort, convenience, and status for equity—even when it's hard.

Correspondences for Inspiration

Consider exploring sources of inspiration that you associate with Justice. To help get you started, here are a few popular connections.

Uranus in Libra, koi fish, eagles, cougars, hares, elephants, mugwort, aloe, iris, gardenia, vanilla, jasmine, moonstone, crystal, aquamarine, sulfates, pearl, scales, swords, calcite, obsidian, beryl, 11:11

✎   What reminds you of Justice? How do these things inspire you to keep going?

How Justice Can Show Up

There are as many interpretations of tarot as there are people who have ever lived. There is no completely universal card interpretation because there is no completely universal perspective on life. Your and your clients' interpretations are what matter the most during a reading. Of all the possible magical ingredients, we humans are the most powerful in enacting real-world change. However, there are strong collective energies around the themes that appear more frequently when a particular archetype shows up. Here are some of those common motifs.

THE BALANCED JUSTICE

- Is straightforward
- Shows prudence
- Exhibits diplomacy
- Remains objective
- Researches before deciding what's true
- Enforces group agreements
- Ends toxic lineages

✎   My relationship to Justice feels balanced when _____

THE IMBALANCED JUSTICE

- Judges harshly
- Has a "cop mentality"
- Doesn't look beyond the surface

- Abuses power
- Chooses tradition over what's right
- Is insensitive
- Exhibits hypocrisy
- Won't accept "what is"

✎ **My relationship to Justice feels imbalanced when** _____

Understanding Capitalism's Racist Foundations

After our journey so far, Justice asks us to sincerely align with our visions and goals, even if they're unpopular, painful, or traditionally deprioritized.

Some readers associate key eleven, the Justice card, with the ancient Egyptian goddess Maat. This deity personifies the concepts of truth, balance, order, harmony, law, morality, and justice. At the very moment of creation, they gracefully cultivate order from chaos.

Ancient Egyptian leaders created the principle of Maat to meet the diverse needs of a growing Egypt, a state that welcomed disparate groups of people with conflicting interests. Maat reflects balance in everything from the universe's nature to social honesty and reciprocity.

For some, Maat represents universal truths about humans' basic needs, including equitable freedom to thrive. These requirements are more important than stalwartly upholding our broken systems for consistency's sake. Maat illustrates how justice is integral to our shared responsibility of community care.

Justice is our work.

Naturally, it can be difficult to imagine life beyond racialized capitalism and mass incarceration. But the responsibility of collective care can empower us to carve new paths for individual and collective thriving. As Rachel Pollack wrote of the Justice card in *Seventy-Eight Degrees of Wisdom*, "We are formed by the actions we have taken in the past; we form our future selves by the actions we take now." Clarity about the past advises how we conceptualize and form new worlds. This may be why the central Justice figure in the Rider-Waite-Smith deck is so alert, fearlessly abandoning the blindfold in the visually similar High Priestess card.

Justice confidently holds the sword of discernment that helps us cut through mistaken or limiting thoughts. Imagining yourself carrying this sword; how do you envision a society beyond the one you're living in?

The year 2020 featured mass rage against government policies and systems that perpetuate racialized violence. Upholding capitalism's racist foundations is critical to its success; its bedrock underpins ways that dominant cultures preserve institutions designed to dehumanize and criminalize people of color. The term "capitalism" is omnipresent in radical discourse, so it's worthwhile to know the origins of this destructive network.

Capitalism requires a hierarchy in which many lose so a few can win. It's a pyramid where the wealthy minority of people uses financial control to exploit their workers, often by cheapening labor while demanding more from employees. Capitalism's prevalence in a largely anti-Black world renders it unsurprising that it harms people of color with less financial power. Even the briefest of gazes into the past reveals how people have long used racism to justify imperialist violence and subjugation. As professors Olúfémi O. Táiwò and Liam Kofi Bright argued in the article "A Response to Michael Walzer," "Racial capitalism is the only sort we've ever had."

In the article "Modern U.S. Racial Capitalism," Charisse Burden-Stelly writes, "Blackness expresses a structural location at the bottom of the labor hierarchy characterized by depressed wages, working conditions, job opportunities, and widespread exclusion from labor unions." This reflects what Karl Marx described as "primitive accumulation," the ways that capitalism relies on extralegal resource extraction and the unfair monitoring and policing of the lower classes. In the *Poverty of Philosophy*, Marx wrote:

> *Slavery is an economic category like any other ... Needless to say we are dealing only with direct slavery, with Negro [sic] slavery in Surinam, in Brazil, in the Southern States of North America. Direct slavery is just as much the pivot of bourgeois industry as machinery, credits, etc. Without slavery you have no cotton; without cotton you have no modern industry. It is slavery that gave the colonies their value; it is the colonies that created world trade, and it is world trade that is the precondition of large-scale industry. Thus slavery is an economic category of the greatest importance.*

It's antihistorical to posit that capitalism's initial rapid expansion was separate from the transatlantic slave commerce. But the connection between capitalism and racism isn't just an issue of the past. It dictates much of our current world, where the ruling class uses racism to maintain domination, influence, and control.

Capitalism creates a small ruling class that oversees a large working class. It requires a divided working class—a small group of powerful people is no match for the massive potential of a unified working class. The dominating class strategically positions laborers against each other to create arbitrary divisions that fragment the working class, such as by stoking white resentment of immigrants of color. Capitalism's beneficiaries create structural and cultural schemes to convince white workers that they are closer to attaining wealth than becoming unhoused to persuade those employees to align their motives and interests with leadership teams, which are often disproportionately white. Deceptions of unity with the ruling class encourage some white workers to attempt to escape class struggles by moving up the ranks at work. Rare is the working-class employee who becomes abundantly wealthy through hard work. At the same time, we recognize how insidiously covert racism supports a workforce in which white people are more likely to receive promotions, often independent of relative effort. Find a picture of your company's executive board and discover who these people are, noting the board's racial composition and learning their backgrounds and qualifications.

White workers substantially benefit from racism. Racism is more than being a bad person or having some prejudices. Racism as a complex system that is the basis of capitalist societies pacifies white workers just enough for them to accept what they have as what they deserve. Racism reinforces how white workers often have access to better jobs, schools, homes, neighborhoods, and community resources. It also reinforces the discrepancies of perceived safety among races. Job security is safety. When accused of similar offenses, white workers are less likely to face discipline than their Black coworkers. Capitalism fortifies racial divisions in offices, factories, and entire industries to splinter the working class, the bottom of the labor pyramid, into disparate factions unlikely to unite and revolt against oppressive forces.

The working class consists of many different identities that reflect income, race, job security, and more. This group isn't homogenous. We must soberly acknowledge and respect our differences in the pursuit of class unity. Nothing about the working class's income, race, or job security will ever align their material interests with those of the wealthy ruling elite. On average, white people enjoy a higher standard of living than Black and Brown people, but white workers have a lot more in common with them than they do with billionaire tycoons. The only ways to become a billionaire are to inherit wealth or exploit laborers.

Only under a collective care model can society see full liberation—yes, only through a society for the majority rather than the power and privilege of a few. Without a ruling class, people of all races could collectively run working spaces, like farms and offices. We could view labor as the maximization of everyone's well-being rather than the generation of profit.

The long history of racism will not immediately disappear after a workers' revolution. In the initial phases of new worlds, we'll likely remember the old ones quite clearly. May we never forget that eliminating the profit-driven and materialistic conditions for capitalism removes many conditions that sustain racism. Economic equity, education access, job opportunities, medical care, and higher standards of living are immediate reasons to disassemble the competitive and exclusionary tenets of capitalism. Does not every child born deserve the eventual choice to thrive?

It's vital to note that Justice goes beyond apples-to-apples fairness principles. Justice is bigger than the imaginary principles by which the dominant classes subjugate people of color around the world.

Close your eyes and envision what an equitable world might look like beyond capitalism. Do you conjure a world of collective responsibility and care? This is the world we deserve.

SUGGESTED EXERCISES

1. Read chapter 1 of Kwame Ture and Charles V. Hamilton's *Black Power: The Politics of Liberation*, titled "White Power: The Colonial Situation."

2. Read Martin Luther King Jr.'s critiques of capitalism, in his own words.

3. Watch or listen to "We Can't Eradicate Racism Without Eradicating Racial Capitalism" on *Democracy Now!* (2 min 35 sec; captioned).

4. Read "What Picketing Taught Me About Feminism" by Julia Carrie Wong.

5. Check out *Capitalism and Slavery* by Eric Williams.

Identifying as Justice

How do you already embody Justice? Use this list of words commonly associated with this card to identify the qualities that you do and don't want to work with as you help create a radically more equitable world.

- Circle the qualities you already embody and can leverage as a superpower.

- Draw a heart around the qualities you want to embody more deeply or frequently.

- Draw a square around the qualities you want to transmute or avoid.

Advocate	Integrity	Alignment	Willing to be called out	Decisive
Servant	Honest	Balanced	Clings to tradition	Cheater
Watches for bias	Philosophy in the mundane	Binary thinking	Compromises	Takes responsibility
Ends harmful patterns	Oblivious to power dynamics	Puts self first	Judgmental	Versatile

Affirmations for Embodying Justice

As you define truth with the Justice card, you might choose an affirmation to motivate you when the work is difficult. Affirmations can strengthen commitment by supporting your confidence in achieving personal and community goals. They can also help combat fear, anxiety, self-doubt, and loss of motivation, which are common feelings that come up in social justice work. You can chant them, write them down, meditate on them, add them to your phone background, or otherwise work with them consistently to keep focused on your objectives. Here are some examples.

"Equality is not the same as equity."

"I accept my consequences."

"I judge because I'm human. I judge compassionately because I'm divine."

"I model what I want to see in others."

"No justice, no peace."

✎ Often, the most powerful affirmations are the ones we create for ourselves. Take some time to jot down your personal affirmations.

Magical Practices to Conjure Justice

Name and respond to how bias affects your work. Hold multiple truths at once. Understand standards and expectations by which you judge other cultures. Forgive yourself. Stop celebrating racist traditions and holidays. Address your organization's internal conflicts. Question your truth regularly. Hold the fire underneath public officials. Become a court advocate. Apologize publicly. Pay reparations. Be accountable to your standards for other people. Support the National Bail Out Collective. Research. Learn about your community's laws. Pull over to be a "just in case" witness when you see a person of color stopped by police. Fight forced labor and wage slavery.

Becoming the Justice Archetype

Meditate on your relationship with Justice and use what you know to plan real-world action. By responding to these prompts, you are committing to doing the work—period.

SET A PERSONAL, RELATIONAL, OR COLLECTIVE INTENTION

✎ Name an objective that your work will center around.

✎ Plan specific actions for this objective that you will take as you embody Justice.

✎ This [day/week/month/event], I will embody Justice in my liberation work by _____

_____

✎ This work is important because _____

✎ The affirmation I will repeat is _____

REFLECT ON YOUR EXPERIENCE

✎ Evolution is iterative and often nonlinear. As we pursue our goals, we must regularly evaluate our actions, mistakes, and learnings to inform the next cycles of change. Review your experience and identify what you can take with you as you move through your antiracism work.

- Successes

- Setbacks

- Frustrations

- Questions

- Other reflections

- Next steps

Demand Reparations

Justice inspires us to give up our privileges so that others can have them. Justice work is equity work, and this archetype dutifully watches how society's scales tip from side to side. One technique to equalize the playing field is making reparations. In "Why We Need Reparations for Black Americans," Rashawn Ray and Andre M. Perry declare:

> *Not only do racial wealth disparities reveal fallacies in the American Dream, the financial and social consequences are significant and wide-ranging. Wealth is positively correlated with better health, educational, and economic outcomes. Furthermore, assets from homes, stocks, bonds, and retirement savings provide a financial safety net for the inevitable shocks to the economy and personal finances that happen throughout a person's lifespan.*

Fair reparations don't erase generations of trauma, but they are a step toward healing the impact of slavery, Jim Crow laws, and mass incarceration on Black people. In a capitalist society, money is power. Reparations offer power, and thus greater freedom, to historically, legally, and culturally disenfranchised people. The Justice archetype holds out a hand to lift people up after they've been knocked to the ground because their privilege is honorless until they share it.

Answer the following questions and strategize how you will support reparations.

1. How does the United States currently profit and otherwise benefit from slavery?

2. What are reparations?

3. What do you know about the history of the reparations movement?

4. What are some ideas about how reparations to Black people might look? Do you have any ideas?

5. What other groups have received reparations from the U.S. government?

6. Specifically, how will you fight for reparations?

12

THE HANGED ONE

Not everything that is faced can be changed;
but nothing can be changed until it is faced.

—JAMES BALDWIN

The Hanged One (key twelve) foreshadows the World (key twenty-one). To better appreciate and understand the world, they routinely view it from a radically fresh perspective. The Hanged One voluntarily suspends themselves upside down to see themselves and the world from another aspect, then uses their fresh observations to pinpoint their next steps toward the world to come. Gaining perspective is the critical work that leads to the next card, Death.

The Hanged One's calm suspension suggests radical acceptance despite discomfort. To accept the right now, they must live in the right now. The Hanged One doesn't fight their inverted position, but rather remains calm while gazing at their familiar yet clearly different surroundings. Physical disorientation might seem like adversity, but this archetype finds peace and hope in knowing that nothing is always as it initially appears at face value.

Key twelve is fully secure in their weirdness. In fact, they *prefer* to be weird. Unafraid of nontraditional positions, the Hanged One persists toward enlightenment despite adversaries who make fun of them, eschew their mission, or scoff at their intentions. They firmly stand for what matters, even when the wind blows the other way.

This archetype also has a simple message: pause. The Hanged One expects a waning moon after a waxing moon and they mimic that cycle by prioritizing rest and reflection after action.

The Hanged One can

- See multiple perspectives
- Sacrifice for overarching goals
- Take regular breaks
- Embrace difficulty
- March to the beat of their own drum
- Identify how their thoughts shape their world
- Serve as a volunteer, nonprofit worker, creative writer, or musician

Embodied Keywords

Pull out the Hanged One from one deck or several. Take a deep breath and pause. Gaze at the imagery. From a liberation perspective, envision yourself in the card's landscape. Be the archetype. Name some keywords that you personally associate with this card. Remember, your definitions are more relevant to your tarot reading than what's in the little white book. Here are a few keywords to help get you started.

Sacred pause, waiting, perspective, passiveness, vulnerability, martyrdom, revelation, relaxation, surrender, calm, epiphany, acceptance, suffering, observance, selflessness, presence, meditation, necessary discomfort, clarification, enlightenment, secrets revealed, ego death, alternatives, breath

Your keywords: _____

The Hanged One in Liberation Work

The Hanged One periodically steps back from their work in order to view it from different perspectives. They practice holographic thinking—that is, they approach issues from different angles, distances, and levels of light and shadow. They're flexible enough to change their worldview when they learn new information. This archetype doesn't need certainty to be comfortable. They spend ample time with the questions, noticing when those questions have more to say than the answers do. They accept that the path of liberation is full of unknowns because they are part of a movement that is building a world no one's ever seen before.

Neptune conjunct Jupiter illustrates how the Hanged One can unveil what's behind Neptune's illusions by seeking the deeper knowledge of Jupiter. This knowledge reveals enigmas (Neptune), allowing the Hanged One to establish related truths (Jupiter). This archetype can symbolize the pursuit of pausing to gain deeper knowledge. The Hanged One isn't always in the streets or at every city council meeting. They must act, but in order to act, they must know. So they learn. The Hanged One researches and reflects, and then researches and reflects deeper and deeper. They listen to and learn from primary sources and a wide variety of other resources. They are activists in a world constantly in motion. The Hanged One is a lifelong learner because up-to-date information makes their work more relevant and thus more effective on a planet that never stops changing.

The Hanged One is intimate with the fact that life is fragile. Death, card thirteen, is around the corner. They know that life is short, and—once they release from their inverted position—they must act with urgency. Sometimes we want to do the right thing, but it's a challenge to do it in a timely fashion. "I'll send mutual aid later this week." "I'll send the email tomorrow." "I'll call back about the grant another day." The Hanged One promptly follows impulses sparked by epiphanies, even if they don't expect immediate results. Mapping Police Violence reports that 24 percent of people killed by police in 2022 were Black. People are dying now. The time for liberation is now. Society does not wait until you feel like a "good activist" or until social justice work becomes convenient for you. Perfect timing is rare, so the Hanged One doesn't expect to act gracefully or flawlessly. The work is often rough, messy, and nonlinear, and this devotion compels us to get our hands dirty.

Correspondences for Inspiration

Consider exploring sources of inspiration that you connect with the Hanged One. To help get you started, here are a few popular associations.

Neptune conjunct Jupiter, midnight, noon, clear quartz, prasiolite, unakite, leopard agate, waterfowl, snakes, scorpions, fish, eagles, water plants, comfrey, willow, ash, myrrh, white tea, ocean mist, hourglass

What reminds you of the Hanged One? How do these things inspire you to keep going?

How the Hanged One Can Show Up

There are as many interpretations of tarot as there are people who have ever lived. There is no completely universal card interpretation because there is no completely universal perspective on life. Your and your clients' interpretations are what matter the most during a reading. Of all the possible magical ingredients, we humans are the most powerful in enacting real-world change. However, there are strong collective energies around the themes that appear more frequently when a particular archetype shows up. Here are some of those common motifs.

THE BALANCED HANGED ONE

- Models patience
- Is present
- Notices how and why things change
- Embraces other philosophies
- Addresses their blind spots
- Brings peace to relationships and gatherings
- Accepts that the work comes with trials

✎ My relationship to the Hanged One feels balanced when _____

THE IMBALANCED HANGED ONE

- Makes hasty decisions
- Disassociates
- Feels unable to move forward
- Procrastinates
- Is unwilling to make sacrifices
- Doesn't believe in themselves
- Overly attaches to their ego

✎ My relationship to the Hanged One feels imbalanced when _____

Sharing the Mic with Intention

We exist in the present moment in a radically new way whenever we adjust our perspective.

One way we can perceive the numerology of the double-digit Major Arcana cards is by examining what happens when the second digit works through the first. With the Hanged One (12), we can address the blind spots in our thinking (Vulcan, represented by 2) through our will (Mars, represented by 1). The Hanged One flows naturally into our antiracism efforts, since this work involves continually checking for and addressing our oversights.

The Hanged One asks us, individually and collectively, to get uncomfortable and to be fully present in our discomfort to discover things we've never noticed. Illumination is the work of the Hanged One.

We can change our perspectives when we pass the mic.

We can't possibly know what it's like to be someone else in every way, and it can sting when someone speaks about your experience as if they were an expert on it. So why do so many white people speak at length with authority on the Black experience without the authority on the Black experience?

If you are white, recall the last race-centric conversation you had. Who wasn't there? Who should have been? Who did everyone get their information from? Who is affected by your conversation?

Passing the mic means letting marginalized people talk about their issues in their own voices. White people need not become shrinking violets and stop talking about racism. Culturally, everyone has different perceptions of permission and safety around speaking up. Instead of paraphrasing another person's story, the Hanged One lets that person take the stage. In mainstream media, we can see how often BIPOC voices are muted, misinterpreted, shamed, and reviled. We can't wait for the media to change their approach. Oppressed people have things to say, and they need to say them now. If we always talk about one thing, what might we learn when someone else speaks on the same topic in a different way? The curious Hanged One looks forward to hear how other people can flip the script. Even when they risk hurt or guilty feelings, this archetype makes space for the voices of people with less access, visibility, or popularity. The Hanged One's inspiration is anything but monolithic.

Our impact on eradicating deeply structural racism points in the right direction when we let the ship be steered by the voices, needs, and stories of those affected. Your favorite social justice activist on Instagram isn't the only person with ideas. Go deeper. Find someone else. Seek voices that speak independently of what white people may consider acceptable speech. If you want the truth, you must accept that it may not arrive in your preferred packaging. Don't just change your perspective, but let your perspective be changed. Let BIPOC tell you what they need to prosper. Social media makes primary sources more accessible than ever before. If you can't recall any firsthand stories, then you're not looking hard enough.

Passing the mic doesn't end after you've handed it off. It continues as also a solemn vow to check your expectations of what comes after. Ask yourself:

- Does this person genuinely want to contribute in the way I'm asking them to?
- Am I imposing on them to be a spokesperson for their racial group(s)?
- Am I only asking one person for one perspective about a many-sided issue? Why?
- How am I compensating for the person's emotional labor?
- How do I know that it's not marginalized people's obligation to decode their oppression for other people?

Share the mic, but do it intentionally. It's everybody's job to notice and unlearn oppressive mindsets and habits. Then we must use our experiences, our perspectives, to help other people notice and unlearn their oppressive mindsets and habits.

After your time upside down, return upright so you can transform revelation into action.

SUGGESTED EXERCISES

1. Do a social media audit, identifying and then acting on how your feeds can more diversely inform and inspire your equity work.

2. Identify your favorite healer, guru, or other spiritual leader. Where do they get their information from? Are their sources diverse? Are their teachings expanding your worldview or simply maintaining it?

3. List ways that you've viewed or referred to Black people as a monolith. What did this compartmentalization do for you? How will you resist future urges to compartmentalize?

4. Research the myth of white exceptionalism.

5. If you're a content creator who works with reviewers, establish a diverse group of people to review your work before you present it and check your blind spots.

6. Subscribe to a Black person's newsletter, open their emails, and read their content.

Identifying as the Hanged One

How do you already embody the Hanged One? Use this list of words commonly associated with this card to identify the qualities that you do and don't want to work with as you help create a radically more equitable world.

- Circle the qualities you already embody and can leverage as a superpower.
- Draw a heart around the qualities you want to embody more deeply or frequently.
- Draw a square around the qualities you want to transmute or avoid.

Listens	Tranquil	Detached	Comfortable with abstract	Humble
Seeks greater knowledge	Hates doing nothing	Tolerant	Wants easy answers	Giving
Stuck in a rut	Outwardly unique	Feels defeated	Stoic	Rushes
Learning blocks	Evaluates	On again, off again	Actively sacrifices privilege	Considers the big picture

Affirmations for Embodying the Hanged One

As you sway with the Hanged One, you might choose an affirmation to motivate you when the work is difficult. Affirmations can strengthen commitment by supporting your confidence in achieving personal and community goals. They can also help combat fear, anxiety, self-doubt, and loss of motivation, which are common feelings that come up in social justice work. You can chant them, write them down, meditate on them, add them to your phone background, or otherwise work with them consistently to keep focused on your objectives. Here are some examples.

"No one can do what I do the way I do it."

"The world is a different place every time I look at it."

"I am change and I am changed."

"I help radically heal the world."

"Pausing reveals options."

✎ **Often, the most powerful affirmations are the ones we create for ourselves. Take some time to jot down your personal affirmations.**

Magical Practices to Conjure the Hanged One

Spend ten minutes each day on reflection. Give away time, money, or other privileges. Take a backseat to marginalized voices. Learn how oppressors justify their abuse to inform strategic responses. Practice metacognition in varied ways. Unstick stuck initiatives. Take a class. Research modern-day lynching. Become more disciplined. Make space for healthy inaction. Mindfully try something new every single week.

Becoming the Hanged One

Meditate on your relationship with the Hanged One, and use what you know to plan real-world action. By responding to these prompts, you are committing to doing the work—period.

SET A PERSONAL, RELATIONAL, OR COLLECTIVE INTENTION

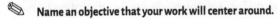 Name an objective that your work will center around.

Plan specific actions for this objective that you will take as you embody the Hanged One.

This [day/week/month/event], I will embody the Hanged One in my liberation work by _____

This work is important because _____

The affirmation I will repeat is _____

REFLECT ON YOUR EXPERIENCE

Evolution is iterative and often nonlinear. As we pursue our goals, we must regularly evaluate our actions, mistakes, and learnings to inform the next cycles of change. Review your experience and identify what you can take with you as you move through your antiracism work.

- Successes
- Setbacks
- Frustrations
- Questions
- Other reflections
- Next steps

Reflect on Your Mistakes

To see the world is to have some sense of the person seeing it (you). With the Hanged One, we look at ourselves from different perspectives to decide our next moves. Retrospection shapes our visions of tomorrow. A shadow aspect of the Hanged One is procrastination. Reflect on the times you've put off action against oppression. Use this space to list examples of what you did and what you could have done instead.

13

DEATH

You wanna fly, you got to give up the shit that weighs you down.

—TONI MORRISON

For a new day to begin, the sun must first set. Death speaks to transformation, the moments of our lives when we end major phases and transition into new forms. Every ending is also a beginning.

The Hanged One identifies what needs to be cleared. Death does the clearing. Nothing lasts forever, and death is inevitable. Keeping this in mind, we can grow less resistant to change. We have no control over the fact that everything in this life ends. We do, however, have control in deciding the bad habits, toxic relationships, nefarious intentions, and other unnecessary baggage we will abandon to lighten tomorrow's load.

We kiss the excess goodbye without completely knowing what's next. The Death card, key thirteen, is the first to go beyond the known, beyond "real" time. (There are twelve months, and midnight and noon prominently demarcate our days.) The Death card gives up problematic habits and relationships without fear of scarcity or abandonment. They channel the oft-feared number 13. We may be familiar with eerie tales about Friday the Thirteenth and serial killers who live on the thirteenth floor. However, some ancient cultures viewed 13 as a sanctified number, a hint of "eternal life." Instead of time completely ending after 11:59 pm, a new day begins. Death is not the final ending; it's an expansion into new spaces. The Death archetype isn't necessarily fearless, but they work through anxiety, doubt, and dread because they believe something greater is around the corner. Everything beyond death is a mystery. The Death card bravely confronts that mystery to pursue something more important than their uneasiness.

Our relationships with the Death card provide opportunities for us to explore our fears and the reasons behind them. What are we afraid of losing? Where do we refuse to release our grips? And why? How do we handle shame and guilt? Death doesn't bypass grief; they reserve time and space to mourn their past selves. The grieving process lubricates the passage from one end to another, incrementally thrusting our transitions toward greater peace and purpose.

In some older decks, the Death card has no name. This card conjures the ineffable, unknowable, and unspeakable beyond. Death is without form, cageless. Death is liberation through surrender. This card clarifies when we can't move on without letting go of something. Each of us has a limited amount of energy. When we clean our energetic houses, we create voids big enough for what we want. We spend less energy clinging onto what pacified our past selves and save it for when more profound or enjoyable elements enter our lives. The process of release can be a battlefield for our egos. We need to surmount guilt and shame to accept that different results require different actions. After conscious release, the next evolutionary phase becomes clearer.

Of course, this card can point to literal death. The Death card's themes of transition into the unknown can soothe and comfort both people dying and those mourning. None of us will live forever, so we might as well tend to the people in our communities while we're here.

The Death archetype can

- Embrace the unknown
- Approach situations without bias
- Let go of bad habits easily
- Know that not all relationships should last forever
- Take risks to pursue new goals
- Show comfort in the shadows
- Serve as a death doula, bookkeeper, electrician, or seamster

Embodied Keywords

Pull out the Death card from one deck or several. Take a deep breath and pause. Gaze at the imagery. From a liberation perspective, envision yourself in the card's landscape. Be the archetype. Name some keywords that you personally associate with this card. Remember, your definitions are more relevant to your tarot reading than what's in the little white book. Here are a few keywords to help get you started.

> Transformation, portals, dreams, impartiality, cycles, liminal spaces, flow, grief, retrospection, cutting cords, void, metamorphic rage, shadow, freedom, ending patterns, cleansing, transition, formlessness, underworld, regeneration, molting, mortality, contrast, inevitability, trauma healing, new approaches, clear vision, humus, time, universality, audacity

✎ **Your keywords:** _____

The Death Card in Liberation Work

The number 13 represents the Death card. Reducing the card by adding its digits shows that Death's teacher card is the Emperor. Some might wonder what the Emperor, a card of construction, has to do with Death, a card of deconstruction. Death gives meaning to the lives we build through Emperor energy. Dying does not render everything we built meaningless. Our limited time to help construct a more equitable society imbues our work with meaning and urgency. We can't wait forever because we don't have forever. But we do have the present, so let's get to work while we can.

Death is a shofar, an alarm clock, a call to awaken. The Judgement card sounds similar, but Death's reveille is more of a reminder that the time for atonement is coming. Prior to reconciliation, they must shed any facades veiling their contributions and abuses. Death encounters their ego head-on and evaluates whether their habits, hang-ups, and addictions are helpful, neutral, or harmful. Then they compost their burdens and use the fertile soil to cultivate greater and more consistent integrity.

Death leads people into the unknown. They've witnessed countless cycles of change and know how to guide their friends, family, communities, and organizations through uncomfortable yet vital revolution. They are a transformation doula. When depicted by Earth in Scorpio, Death (Scorpio) metamorphoses substance (Earth) to create new life. This card leverages change as a bridge to something better. This card leaves toxic people and practices, reallocating energy to efforts that improve the world. It's about sitting in grief and showing up for grievers. This card prioritizes life and protects Black bodies. It's the new vibe you emanate that shows your peers that times have changed. Death finds possibility where others see a desert. Death is change. Death is a butterfly.

Correspondences for Inspiration

Consider exploring sources of inspiration that you associate with the Death card. To help get you started, here are a few popular correspondences.

> Scorpio season, salt, reproductive organs, Friday the 13th, lunar cycles, skin, elder, yew, blackthorn, cactus, water forget-me-nots, scorpions, bat, wolf, scarab beetle, vulture, Pluto, copal resin, sundials, pinecones, dark moon

✎ What reminds you of the Death card? How do these things inspire you to keep going?

How the Death Card Can Show Up

There are as many interpretations of tarot as there are people who have ever lived. There is no completely universal card interpretation because there is no completely universal perspective on life. Your and your clients' interpretations are what matter the most during a reading. Of all the possible magical ingredients, we humans are the most powerful in enacting real-world change. However, there are strong collective energies around the themes that appear more frequently when a particular archetype shows up. Here are some of those common motifs.

THE BALANCED DEATH ARCHETYPE

- Commits to personal and group evolution
- Takes minimalist approaches
- Knows when to burn bridges

- Will take risks by letting go
- Pays attention to their ego
- Is comfortable speaking about taboo subjects
- Performs righteous rage

✎ My relationship to the Death archetype feels balanced when _____

THE IMBALANCED DEATH ARCHETYPE

- Wants consistently concrete answers
- Does the exact same routine every day
- Considers life meaningless
- Ignores the present by fixating on the past
- Feels stagnant
- Claims powerlessness over their habits
- Clings to people they've outgrown

✎ My relationship to the Death archetype feels imbalanced when _____

Decriminalizing Sex Work as Antiracism

After the Hanged One evolves their perception, it becomes easier to identify what must die out to allocate space for even more radical transformation.

The Death card, key thirteen, often corresponds to Scorpio, the ruler of birth, death, transmutation, and—of course—sex. This archetype reminds us that these things aren't to be feared, but rather understood.

There is a French phrase, *la petite mort*, that generally translates to "the little death." People use the term to refer to sexual orgasms or other postcoital sensations. This phrase literally relates to the Death card, but the connection is also metaphorical. In *Numerology and the Divine Triangle*, Dusty Bunker and Faith Javane name "the mouth of the uterus" as one symbol for this card.

Many societies posit sex as a complicated, heavy subject. In a world where anti-Blackness exists on nearly every continent, it's predictable that many of the sex lives of Black people have long been ogled, overpoliced, reviled, feared, and caricatured. The spotlight intensifies with Black sex workers. Amnesty International describes this reality, stating

> *Sex work is criminalized throughout the United States, typically as misdemeanor offenses. Similar to the way the United States treats and criminalizes drug use, the policing of sex work exacerbates stigma, compromises access to resources, justifies violence, and is steeped in racial disparities. Women of color, especially Black cisgender and transgender women, girls, and femmes, are particularly vulnerable. Because sex work and sex trafficking are conflated, interventions are focused on abolishing the sex industry instead of eliminating structural issues that drive exploitation.*

There are myriad negative consequences to the criminalization of Black sex workers' survival, including higher rates of violence (reported and unreported), exploitation, sexually transmitted infections, and the unfortunately long-lasting consequences of arrest records. Compounded with the fact that Black communities are already overpoliced, Black sex workers' lives are particularly in danger of police abuse.

A report by the Sex Workers Outreach Project stated that Black women only accounted for 2.8 percent of California's population in 2015, but represented 42 percent of all sex work-related arrests. According to the New York State Division of Criminal Justice Services, 85 percent of the people arrested for sex work between 2012 and 2015 were Black or Latinx. This isn't just the picture for these two states—Black sex workers, often women, are targeted by the police in many communities at a far higher rate than their white counterparts. The numbers grow wearier for those who are Black, trans, and femme.

The Death card invites us to acknowledge what we fear out of ignorance and to do whatever it takes to move past our anxieties.

Dropped charges aren't enough for sex workers. Having an arrest record often places a target on sex workers' backs. Police trail these people until they can catch them in sex work–adjacent situations. Sarah Marchando, a Latina and cisgender woman, shared of her experience in the *Village Voice*, "I felt like I was being watched." The NYPD reported seeing her "beckon to multiple vehicles passing by with male drivers," "approach a vehicle," and "engage in conversation with a male inside of said vehicle." Law enforcement used this information to assert that Marchando intended to engage in sex work. The Death card evokes cyclicity. Once a sex worker is documented in the system, law enforcement often works to keep them in it. It's easier for them to justify abuses of power when the victims are already overlooked, marginalized, and dehumanized by the prudish expectations of women established by cishet white supremacist cultures.

The Stop Enabling Sex Trafficking Act (SESTA) and Fight Online Sex Traffickers Act (FOSTA) have significantly endangered sex workers since the bills were introduced in 2018. Proponents claimed that the bills intended to thwart sex trafficking; however SESTA and FOSTA created more hazardous work environments for people who autonomously choose sex work. For example, now there is less access to safe online networks for vetting potential clients, so many sex workers have had to move their work to the streets or other unsafe venues, increasing the likelihood of sexual assault and violence.

At the same time, law enforcement often does not investigate harm against sex workers. For example, the LAPD marked files "No Human Involved" in response to reports of sex worker violence. This deliberate oversight and active prejudice are omnipresent. The fact that there are very limited statistics on violence against sex workers of color speaks to the dehumanization of a group that uses their body for labor, a group not unlike construction workers or people who strain their eyes at a computer all day.

Dehumanization precipitates death.

In 2015 alone, forty-one sex worker deaths were reported (though the number is likely much higher). Seventeen of them were Black and twelve were transgender women. Many victims never see justice meted out to their abusers. The blatant refusal to decriminalize consensual sex labor especially jeopardizes the lives of marginalized sex workers. Who protects the unprotected?

All people deserve to be in control of their bodies and to live self-determined lives free from exploitation. When confronting society's animosity toward sex workers, we must reckon with the fact that race is often a factor in the victimization of and violence against sex laborers. Even if you have never engaged in this type of work, the fight still matters. We live in a world where people are praised for masquerading as sex workers and actual sex workers are murdered as their survival strategies are under constant surveillance and attack.

Work, in general, is something that makes us vulnerable—to the whims of our bosses, opinions of our colleagues, political powers shaping the economy, and beyond. Our livelihoods often depend on exposing ourselves to other people. A human is a human, and humans need safety and freedom to thrive. Nothing about a person's job makes them less deserving of protection and autonomy. If you believe it does, consider how you attach others' jobs to their identities. We are more than our jobs, and our station in life does not change our right to security.

Maybe today, you can become more open to

- Checking your and others' judgment of sex workers
- Being a watchful advocate in situations that might lead to police abuse or other types of sex worker violence
- Meaningfully involving sex workers in equity work and community building
- Respecting sex workers' choices, autonomy, and boundaries
- Paying attention to the language you use to describe sex work

How can we not fight for sex workers' humanness, safety, involvement, and respect, when we fight for everyone to have these things in a more equitable world? Pretending death doesn't exist doesn't make it disappear. Pretending sex workers are subhuman doesn't make them disappear. We're only free once the most marginalized people are free. Thus none of us are free until Black trans femme sex workers are free.

SUGGESTED EXERCISES

Aside from redistributing wealth by sending money to Black sex workers, I invite you to delve very deeply and intentionally into one or more of the following written resources.

1. Learn about the Sex Workers Outreach Project.

2. *Rights Not Rescue: How to Be a Meaningful Ally to Sex Workers* by SWOP-USA

3. "White Feminism, White Supremacy, White Sex Workers" by Juniper Fitzgerald

4. Information on the International Day to End Violence Against Sex Workers

5. *Meaningful Work: Transgender Experiences in the Sex Trade* by Erin Fitzgerald, Sarah Elspeth Patterson, Darby Hickey, Cherno Biko, and Harper Jean Tobin

6. *Revolting Prostitutes: The Fight for Sex Workers' Rights* by Juno Mac and Molly Smith

7. *Hands Up: A Systematized Review of Policing Sex Workers in the U.S.* by Fabian Luis Fernandez

Identifying as the Death Card

How do you already embody the Death card? Use this list of words commonly associated with this card to identify the qualities that you do and don't want to work with as you help create a radically more equitable world.

- Circle the qualities you already embody and can leverage as a superpower.
- Draw a heart around the qualities you want to embody more deeply or frequently.
- Draw a square around the qualities you want to transmute or avoid.

Facilitates endings	Thrives in ambiguity	Denial	Avoids reality	Conservative
Hoards	Waning hope	Evolution	Difficulty moving on	Energy vampire
Eager to grow	Baggage	Witness	Inspires change in others	Minimalist
Stagnant	Self-destruction	Hopelessness	Cutting cords	Honors grief

Affirmations for Embodying the Death Archetype

Transforming alongside the Death archetype, you might choose an affirmation to motivate you when the work is difficult. Affirmations can strengthen commitment by supporting your confidence in achieving personal and community goals. They can also help combat fear, anxiety, self-doubt, and loss of motivation, which are common feelings that come up in social justice work. You can chant them, write them down, meditate on them, add them to your phone background, or otherwise work with them consistently to keep focused on your objectives. Here are some examples.

"The person I used to be is not the person I need to be today."

"I forgive myself."

"Memento mori."

"Out of the void, I create myself."

"I will only carry what I can support."

✎ Often, the most powerful affirmations are the ones we create for ourselves. Take some time to jot down your personal affirmations.

Magical Practices to Conjure the Death Card

Defend Black women and femmes. Donate menstrual products. Remove monuments of hate. Hold space for grieving people. Do something when you see police brutality, physical or otherwise. Build something temporary in service of something bigger. Reuse materials. Protect native plants. Dream bigger. Repurpose an old building instead of demolishing it. Embody benevolent ancestors. Protect sunrises and sunsets by fighting pollution. Become a hospice volunteer. Confront one fear every day. Learn about death rituals across cultures. Donate tissue. Fund addiction counseling. Reconnect with what makes living feel worthwhile even though it is temporary. Fund rematriation projects.

Becoming the Death Archetype

Meditate on your relationship with the Death archetype and use what you know to plan real-world action. By responding to these prompts, you are committing to doing the work—period.

SET A PERSONAL, RELATIONAL, OR COLLECTIVE INTENTION

✎ Name an objective that your work will center around.

✎ Plan specific actions for this objective that you will take as you embody the Death card.

✎ This [day/week/month/event], I will embody the Death card in my liberation work by _____

✎ This work is important because _____

✎ The affirmation I will repeat is _____

REFLECT ON YOUR EXPERIENCE

✎ Evolution is iterative and often nonlinear. As we pursue our goals, we must regularly evaluate our actions, mistakes, and learnings to inform the next cycles of change. Review your experience and identify what you can take with you as you move through your antiracism work.

- Successes

- Setbacks

- Frustrations

- Questions

- Other reflections

- Next steps

Say Their Names

The Death card calls us to appreciate our temporary mortality. Unfortunately, some of us only think about it when we hear that someone has died. The reality of death isn't far from many Black minds with the frequency of reports about Black victims of police violence.

Today, face death. List thirteen Black people murdered by the police; then list facts about them that are unrelated to their deaths. Who was their favorite relative? What did they want to be when they grew up? What did they do with their free time? The list of these people is long, but it is never a monolith. Remember that behind the news stories, people murdered by police were humans with feelings, ambitions, and passions. May they rest in peace and may we commit our work to their memory.

14

TEMPERANCE

If art doesn't make us better, then what on earth is it for?

—ALICE WALKER

Temperance, the "art card," illuminates our inner alchemist as we turn loss into something bigger, something more beautiful. Key fourteen completes the second line of the Major Arcana, and here we culminate, as it reflects back to us a montage of our inner evolution. Temperance prepares to enter the land of the superconscious by collaging disparate parts of themselves into a unique identity. This convergence is art, life art. As a painter alchemizes by blending colors, Temperance demonstrates how we manipulate the current reality into something better. There's no one right way to create art. Temperance finds their style through conscious experimentation.

Temperance and the Magician are both alchemists but Temperance doesn't need tools like the Magician does. Without precise instructions, they bravely moderate their magic through direct access, elucidating their most potent source of magic: themselves. Like the Chariot who concluded the line of the ego before diving into the interior, Temperance sets the stage for the Major Arcana's third line by reinventing themselves again—this time especially for the greater collective. They check in with various parts of their personalities and make bold changes where needed. Temperance can't afford not to—they cast the spell, they live the spell, they *are* the spell.

Temperance, key fourteen, emerges from the Death card's clearing with nothing but what is essential for the spiral road ahead. In some interpretations of the Egyptian myth of Osiris, his body is cut into fourteen pieces and reconnected before resurrection. The fourteen pieces represent the fourteen days of a waning moon before it begins to rebuild into fullness. This story asks: what can survive death? After death, Temperance is purer in intention and dedication. Now it is time for them to embody these changes. They no longer fear death because it's given them more freedom and agency to deal with the Devil and the Tower. After Temperance makes it through the fire, they convert the ashes into ink: they begin writing a new story.

The Temperance archetype can

- Turn trash into treasure
- Participate enthusiastically in their own healing
- Practice everyday magic
- Bring multiple people together for a single cause
- Manage resources without hoarding them
- Protect others' individuality
- Serve as a cook or barista, waste collector, lawyer, herbalist, chemist, or street artist

Embodied Keywords

Pull out the Temperance card from one deck or several. Take a deep breath and pause. Gaze at the imagery. From a liberation perspective, envision yourself in the card's landscape. Be the archetype. Name some keywords that you personally associate with this card. Remember, your definitions are more relevant to your tarot reading than what's in the little white book. Here are a few keywords to help get you started.

> Reconstitution, magic, curiosity, balance, synergy, reexamination, nudity, coordination, deeper purpose, foraging, return, kintsugi, alignment, tranquility, worlds beyond binaries, metamorphosis, experimentation, reinvention, divine assistance, rebirth, self-restraint, internal resources, bravery, flow

 Your keywords: _____

Temperance in Liberation Work

Themes of balance run throughout the Major Arcana. The Lovers seek internal equilibrium, Justice looks for it externally. Temperance does both.

Temperance inspires us to get in touch with our humanity so we can see it in others. When we lift veils with Death's guidance, we remove clutter that obscures what we truly are: humans navigating life by balancing convictions and discernment. Aware of the risks of extremism, Temperance artfully harmonizes the types and amount of energy they bring to their movement. Some situations require hard-core action; at other times we need to fall back. Temperance reads the room and knows how to act in discussions where they're not a subject-matter expert.

The Temperance archetype simultaneously dons multiple hats. Temperance is a mirror that reveals our true selves for the compassion, knowledge, tools, and talents that they can offer movements. Their community action toolkit doesn't look like anybody else's, evidence that it's their privilege and responsibility to use it. They're the forest ranger who watches kids during protests. They're the cashier who learned graphic design when their financially strapped organization needed it. They're the accountant who monitors the budget and teaches sign language on weeknights. Temperance capitalizes on their multifaceted nature and ardently seeks ways to participate, even when the tasks aren't in their usual wheelhouse. They're creative enough to make it work.

Temperance romances experimentation. With the Death card, they eliminated or transmuted bad ideas and failed experiments. This archetype isn't afraid to try wild ideas—and fail. It takes both small everyday actions and broad, sweeping changes to craft a more equitable planet. Temperance will never know the efficacy of their ideas until they try them. Through open-minded iteration, they alchemize creative ideas into concrete actions.

Correspondences for Inspiration

Consider exploring sources of inspiration that you connect with the Temperance card. To help get you started, here are a few popular associations.

Sagittarius, oud, agarwood, lime, pimpernel, mulberries, oak, birch trees, centaurs, dogs, horses, elk, topaz, jacinth, amethyst, rivers, Jupiter, mirrors, shores, endless knots, theta binaural beats, quilts, irises

 What reminds you of the Temperance card? How do these things inspire you to keep going?

How the Temperance Card Can Show Up

There are as many interpretations of tarot as there are people who have ever lived. There is no completely universal card interpretation because there is no completely universal perspective on life. Your and your clients' interpretations are what matter the most during a reading. Of all the possible magical ingredients, we humans are the most powerful in enacting real-world change. However, there are strong collective energies around the themes that appear more frequently when a particular archetype shows up. Here are some of those common motifs.

THE BALANCED TEMPERANCE ARCHETYPE

- Is ready to go deeper
- Evolves personality with experience
- Performs embodied spells
- Integrates their mission into everyday life
- Identifies potential intersections
- Shares art without worrying about judgment
- Brings people together

 My relationship to the Temperance archetype feels balanced when _____

THE IMBALANCED TEMPERANCE ARCHETYPE

- Lives a highly compartmentalized life
- Performs reckless extremism
- Is wounded

- Has incongruous values
- Bottlenecks
- Litters (energetically or literally)
- Misses their old self

✎ **My relationship to the Temperance archetype feels imbalanced when** _____

Amplify Creative Resistance

The Temperance card meets us at the end of the Major Arcana's interior journey. Here, we return from the Death card's trials with a newfound sense of freedom. We've let a thing go and our Fool's knapsack is a little lighter.

Freedom to choose,
freedom to invent,
freedom to put the pieces
back together in
different ways.

Temperance calls us to craft the lives we want to live and the worlds we want to live in. This is the creative process of life art. Our art is different every time we return to the canvas simply because, even in the slightest, we're not the same person we were last time.

Temperance tempers—combines, extracts, balances—disparate elements, polarities, paradoxes, sounds, materials, textures, interactions, words, movements, states of mind, and perceptions—a kintsugian dream—to rise from Death's ashes in their unique way. This is alchemy. This is wabi-sabi. This is art.

Despite generational trauma, Black art continues to survive and evolve as a powerful force of reflection, resistance, and recreation. Pause and consider its endurance for a few moments.

During the transatlantic slave trade, white enslavers attempted to strip Black people of many things, including their culture. Forced into the lowest bellies of ships, enslaved Africans who didn't share languages or cultures were densely packed together. This wasn't an act of laziness or efficiency—it was intentional. White enslavers filled ships with people with varying cultures to prevent communication, particularly so enslaved people would not unite and revolt. But Black people still invented covert ways to preserve some cultural traditions laying the groundwork for African American culture. Black art persists and thrives, even in white-dominant societies. Pause to consider what that means and looks like in modern cultures.

You might have thought about Betye Saar, Gwendolyn Brooks, Big K.R.I.T., Kehinde Wiley, or Amanda Gorman. You might have thought about a lot of Black creatives.

Despite its wide presence, the elitist, white-dominant art world continues to devalue, censor, and obscure Black art. This is true about music, painting, photography, acting, and plenty of other artforms. Making and funding Black art are political acts of resistance, even when the intended audience is nonwhite.

Like a leaf paradoxically falling from Mercury, these words gently land in our laps: art changes the world and how we see it. We limit our equity work when we deprioritize creativity. Ignoring the power and potential of art denies our movements' communication forms that can touch and inspire people in ways that news articles can't.

Learn the story of how the silhouette of a fist became a symbol of Black power. It's a simple image, but also a widely accessible and highly visible symbol to show support and remind others that our movements are still active. We can see parallels of how art can fuel and help sustain social change at various levels of scale. Consider T. V. Reed's list from *The Art of Protest* about how the arts can transform societies. Art

- Encourages social change
- Empowers and deepens commitment
- Informs the larger society about social issues
- Harmonizes social activists within the movement
- Reinforces values and ideas within movements
- Shifts emotional tones
- Critiques movement ideology
- Provides pleasure and joy

Are these qualities not what our antiracism work needs? So long as oppressive forces uphold racist systems and institutions, art endures as a critical tool for social transformation and cultural competency. The intersection between activism and art has long played a substantial role in the pursuit of justice. Whether through film, music, collage, street art, posters, live demonstration, clay, or another medium, art is a channel through which we can passionately communicate our social justice intentions.

So whose art will you elevate? What art will you create? What art can you share meaningfully?

Media and word of mouth are spreading faster than ever. It is a radical and alchemical act to make or publicize art that subverts white dominance in highly visible ways. No two artists think alike, and no two pieces of art evoke the exact same feelings from every person who experience them. To share art is to inspire as many perspective shifts as there are observers.

Making and sharing art are a spell. Art is the alchemy of collaging different materials, modalities, polarities, paradoxes, sounds, textures, interactions, words, movements, states of mind, and perceptions to transform a canvas. And planet Earth is our shared canvas.

By nature, being human means we are all inherently creative. We require creativity to invent new, unfamiliar worlds. We create, iterate, and share. What parts of your personality can you combine to help cultivate communities where all people who want to make art have the space, time, energy, and resources to do so? Art is about changing the world, but it's about enjoying it too.

SUGGESTED EXERCISES

1. Read "The 'Art World' Can't Exist in a Decolonized Future" by Angie Jaime.

2. Read "Why Is Black Portraiture So Popular Today?" by Shantay Robinson.

3. View the "African American Art: Harlem Renaissance, Civil Rights Era, and Beyond" slideshow hosted on Google Arts & Culture.

4. Learn about the Black Arts Movement. Then intuitively choose an artist or artwork you've never heard of from the movement and go deeper by

learning more about them/it. Keep the lens of your equity work nearby for inspiration or motivation.

5. Check out the "Normalize Teaching That Black Women Pioneered American Music" thread on Instagram.

6. Explore the Black Art in America website and sign up for their newsletter.

7. Learn about the role of music in the struggle against slavery.

8. Order or borrow a copy of *The New Black Vanguard* by Antwaun Sargent.

9. If you're into Southern rap (or if you're not!), catch up on *Bottom of the Map* podcast episodes.

10. Buy a Black artist lunch.

Identifying as the Temperance Card

How do you already embody the Temperance card? Use this list of words commonly associated with this card to identify the qualities that you do and don't want to work with as you help create a radically more equitable world.

-   Circle the qualities you already embody and can leverage as a superpower.
-   Draw a heart around the qualities you want to embody more deeply or frequently.
-   Draw a square around the qualities you want to transmute or avoid.

Long-term vision	Reflection	Intuition	Dogmatism	Coordination
Spiritual bypassing	Cooperation	Concentration	Overindulgence	Competition
Unresolved conflicts	Excessive	Protected	Clear purpose	Secrets
Insecurity	Works well with others	Binary	Inner guidance	Grounded

Affirmations for Embodying Temperance

While making magic with the Temperance archetype, you might choose an affirmation to motivate you when the work is difficult. Affirmations can strengthen commitment by supporting your confidence in achieving personal and community goals. They can also help combat fear, anxiety, self-doubt, and loss of motivation, which are common feelings that come up in social justice work. You can chant them, write them down, meditate on them, add them to your phone background, or otherwise work with them consistently to keep focused on your objectives. Here are some examples.

"Life is art."

"The right way is not always the middle way."

"It takes all kinds to make the earth go around."

"I am the painter, the paintbrush, and the painting."

"I'm safe to try something different."

✎ Often, the most powerful affirmations are the ones we create for ourselves. Take some time to jot down your personal affirmations.

Magical Practices to Conjure Temperance

Donate to local art programs. Craft a zine featuring the voices of marginalized people. Return to the roots of your movement. Ask for help because your mission is bigger than your ego. Explore the politics behind how your town is designed. Reunite families. Review and diversify your news sources. Call out spiritual bypassing. Practice what you preach wherever you go. Fund transitional housing. Elevate trans voices. Speak people's names in rooms where they don't have a seat at the table.

Becoming the Temperance Archetype

Meditate on your relationship with Temperance and use what you know to plan real-world action. By responding to these prompts, you are committing to doing the work—period.

SET A PERSONAL, RELATIONAL, OR COLLECTIVE INTENTION

✎   Name an objective that your work will center around.

✎   Plan specific actions for this objective that you will take as you embody the Temperance card.

✎   This [day/week/month/event], I will embody the Temperance card in my liberation work by _____

✎   This work is important because _____

✎   The affirmation I will repeat is _____

REFLECT ON YOUR EXPERIENCE

✎   Evolution is iterative and often nonlinear. As we pursue our goals, we must regularly evaluate our actions, mistakes, and learnings to inform the next cycles of change. Review your experience and identify what you can take with you as you move through your antiracism work.

- Successes

- Setbacks

- Frustrations

- Questions

- Other reflections

- Next steps

Create Protest Art

Temperance is the card of art, and art can be a powerful tool of revolution. Protest art fosters relationships, establishes shared languages, cultivates community, evokes emotion, and wakes people up when starkly contrasted against mundane backdrops. It also offers us a bigger toolkit of modalities for people to engage with social movements. What might this mean for you? Use the following prompts to guide your discovery.

Explore the role of art in justice movements of today and the past; then describe how you can use art as an asset in your fight toward equity.

What are some powerful examples of protest art?

What are some specific ways that art has progressed various causes?

How might wider access to the arts impact your community?

How can you or your organization use art to take your anti-oppression mission further?

15

THE DEVIL

I'm a firm believer that language and how we use language
determines how we act, and how we act then determines
our lives and other people's lives.

—NTOZAKE SHANGE

The Devil card is the liberation card is the lightbringer card. Through the Devil, we actively and compassionately free ourselves from what thwarts our pursuit of an awakening. The first card in the Major Arcana's third row, key fifteen is the gateway to enlightenment. We must draw nearer to our shadows to turn on the lights.

Embodying the Devil means to release the self from addictive devils—the self-imposed chains we keep wearing out of comfort, convenience, and vice. With Death, we got rid of the unnecessary; the Devil is the alluring force that pulls us back to those things. Capitalism thrives because it successfully convinces billions of people that what they need is external. The Devil appears when we are truly ready to confront the demons in the things that tell us we're not enough. When we remove our shackles, we realize that we're still alive. We never needed past fixations to feel alive. Our spark isn't out there—in relationships, in a career, at the bottom of a bottle—it's been within us all along. The Devil says it's time to get over your shame and truly harness your intrinsic personal power. You can't meaningfully evolve without it.

The Devil doesn't only shine light on detrimental passions; it also shows us the positive ones that give our life flavor. Just like harmful habits, asceticism detracts from the enjoyment of life. The Devil is wild, free, and shameless. Consider your passions or desires that you feel shameful about because of what your friends, family, or communities say. Do they actually cause harm, or are they just "not cool"? It's time to own your desires, to let your freak flag fly. To wield our personal power in the collective, we must get real and confront our innermost desires. What keeps us chained? Only you can define enlightenment for yourself. It becomes easier to realize our inherent wholeness after the Devil's fire razes the things that distract us from our authentic selves. Mizuta Masahide wrote, "Barn's burnt down—now I can see the moon." Habits may be hard to break, but what's beyond them may be the light we've long searched for.

The Devil archetype can

- End unhealthy cycles
- Handle temptation well
- Free people from their prisons
- Show pride in their unique interests
- Have immense ambition
- Channel their innate wildness
- Serve as a dominatrix, self-employed professional, victim advocate, or addiction counselor

Embodied Keywords

Pull out the Devil card from one deck or several. Take a deep breath and pause. Gaze at the imagery. From a liberation perspective, envision yourself in the card's landscape. Be the archetype. Name some keywords that you personally associate with this card. Remember, your definitions are more relevant to your tarot reading than what's in the little white book. Here are a few keywords to help get you started.

> Compassionate liberation, power dynamics, dependency and codependency, light, sexuality, fear, materialism, pleasure, desire, addiction, guilt, uncivilization, gatekeeping, self-punishment, propaganda, breaking patterns, debt, illusions, unlearning, consent, self-understanding, human fallibility, options, truth

 **Your keywords:** _____

The Devil in Liberation Work

No one reaches enlightenment without first getting raw and dirty. The Devil's work is liberation work, and that requires a willingness to call ourselves out for our deepest, darkest compulsions and fixations. Exalted in Venus in Capricorn, the Devil remembers that they are human: imperfect beings who can suffer from things that hold power over them.

When we add the digits of key fifteen, we reconnect with the Lovers. The Devil card can portray 5 (Mercury) working with 1 (Mars) to produce 6: the Lovers card, the card of choice. The ability to process information about our conscious and subconscious minds enables us to choose how we take liberatory action in the material world. The Lovers remind us to consider our relationships with ourselves and independently choose the lives we want to lead. The Devil arrives to help us confront what's blocking the power from living out our informed choices. Here, we confront the obstructions between us and our ability to give marginalized people more choices in life.

The Devil as activist knows what they want out of the world they help build, and they choose to do the work accordingly. They confront their darkest truths, the ways they perpetuate oppression through the practices they can't seem to release. The Devil may unintentionally cause harm when they think they have no other options. Every day, people who pursue freedom still participate in societal oppression because they have to afford to live. Everyone needs nourishment, shelter, and clothing. We might disapprove of capitalism, but we still need to buy food. Even while participating in an oppressive society, we can still strive to reduce harm. The Devil's light illuminates where we do have agency when we think we have none.

The Devil knows addiction. Addiction is often cyclical: initial action, abuse, tolerance, dependence, addiction, relapse, and repeat. The Devil halts cycles of abuse after realizing they have the control to end control. They've become intimate enough with their personal power to gallantly confront how they and society control marginalized people through fear, othering, domination, corruption, exploitation, and shame.

Correspondences for Inspiration

Consider exploring sources of inspiration that you associate with the Devil card. To help get you started, here are a few popular correspondences.

> Venus in Capricorn, ruby, chrysoprase, turquoise, black diamond, onyx, elephant, mountain goats, donkeys, hemp, thyme, dock, poppy, sweet woodruff, willow, thistle, musk, civets, benzoin

✎ **What reminds you of the Devil card? How do these things inspire you to keep going?**

How the Devil Card Can Show Up

There are as many interpretations of tarot as there are people who have ever lived. There is no completely universal card interpretation because there is no completely universal perspective on life. Your and your clients' interpretations are what matter the most during a reading. Of all the possible magical ingredients, we humans are the most powerful in enacting real-world change. However, there are strong collective energies around the themes that appear more frequently when a particular archetype shows up. Here are some of those common motifs.

THE BALANCED DEVIL ARCHETYPE

- Reclaims their power
- Moderates themselves
- Is comfortable with delayed gratification
- Reads the fine print in contracts
- Separates personal standards from societal standards
- Knows what they want
- Helps others get free
- Perseveres

✎ **My relationship to the Devil archetype feels balanced when** _____

- Gives in to temptation easily
- Is tied up in excessive debt or contractual obligations
- Exhibits codependency
- Has an unjustified victim mentality
- Demonstrates possessiveness
- Prefers blissful ignorance
- Stays in unhealthy situations for too long

✎ My relationship to the Devil archetype feels imbalanced when _____

Decentering White Feelings

What holds power over us? What do we hold power over? What do we do with our devils? We have numerous options.

The Devil is a complex figure, and vice is only one of its traits. Imagine if, like in the Slutist Tarot deck, the Death archetype was renamed "Vice." Now define the word without looking it up. One view suggests that it's what we needlessly hold on to. What's your perspective?

After leaving Temperance's oasis, we feel like we've learned all we need to know. We've transformed our inner and outer selves with rigorous devotion and our lives will never be the same. We now know enough to be a "good antiracist," right? Somehow charmingly, the Devil snarls, "Look harder."

Get in front of a mirror and confess to yourself what you've been refusing to give up. Most of us are holding on to something blocking us from escalating our racial justice efforts. It could be your racist boyfriend or a matter of convenience. With the Devil, we release harmful attachments to unlock the gate of more intimate alignment with our integrity. We know when we're doing something wrong. What are your favorite excuses?

The Devil appears when we have the strength and experience to remove the chains we voluntarily shackled around our necks. We harness the power of our inner selves and communities. Naked, we sit patiently with the uneasiness of change. Then we decide to keep, transmute, or shed our vices.

One pervasive white vice is the urge to center themselves in antiracism work. They might mean well, but white self-centering obscures and obfuscates the voices of the people of color they've pledged to elevate. Intent matters, but not more than impact.

Facing a door that makes us uneasy, leaving is always a choice. This option appeals to white people who think they've gone far enough in their antiracism efforts. They've experienced profound feelings and realizations and are excited to ramble stories and emotions without consent of their audience. The more they do this, the more their feelings become the focal point of conversations about race. Regardless of intent, centering white feelings is antithetical to racial equity. It's a multipronged tool white people use to feel comfortable and seen. If you're in the habit of derailing conversations to insert your uninvited story about race, this is a good time to practice the discomfort of verbal restraint.

In "When Feminism Is White Supremacy in Heels," Rachel Cargle names self-centering as the "most common" of all toxic white feminist behaviors:

> White women get so caught up in how they feel in a moment of Black women expressing themselves that they completely vacuum the energy, direction, and point of the conversation to themselves and their feelings. They start to explain why race is hard for them to talk about, what they think would be a better solution to the topic at hand, and perhaps what women of color can do to make it more palatable.

White people are not the center of the world to come.

The Devil invites us to deconstruct the excuses we use to justify unethical behavior. When antiracism becomes uncomfortable for white people, some drop off, focus on low-effort/high-convenience work, fall back into old habits, or return to more insular motivations. "This action is easy; that action is not." Societies around the world circle white stories from the television to the courtroom. This is what many of us are used to. But familiarity isn't an excuse to minimize Black voices because you want everyone to know you care. You don't need to prove your dedication; just show up, listen, and participate.

If you are white, recall the last time you centered yourself in liberation work. What was the context? Was it during an intimate conversation? Were you in a group Slack thread? Was it during a team meeting?

If you're unfamiliar with the concept, examples of white centering are

- Inserting stories into unrelated conversations in response to an unrelated conversation
- Documenting justice work on social media to elicit attention or praise
- Choosing their comfort over others' humanity
- Defending harmful behavior instead of listening, learning, and atoning
- Resisting the responsibility of losing privilege so others can gain it
- Refusing to hold themselves or other white people accountable
- Asserting authority on antiracism topics, thus blocking learning and listening opportunities

White centering is a common vice that deters community progress. People may mean well, but the erasure of Black voices is violence in a time when people of color are suffocated after speaking their minds.

Keep yourself in check and watch the center. If you're unsure where to begin, start with these questions before speaking out:

How does this add to the conversation?

Am I saying this to absolve myself of guilt?

Am I saying this to elevate my status or visibility?

Do I seek sympathy or empathy in a space that isn't mine?

Am I mostly talking about myself?

Am I changing the topic? Why?

Do I need others to know I've done a good thing? What's the benefit?

Am I suggesting how marginalized people should think, behave, or feel?

Would the story I'm sharing matter if I wasn't a part of it?

Am I overshadowing someone with a different experience than mine?

When we pause after the impulse to return to an old habit, breathe deeply before trying something new, or consider potential repercussions before acting, we allow ourselves to check in with our ethics before prioritizing familiarity. When the Devil asks us to plunge deeper, we accept the challenge because we trust the results to be more significant than our sacrifices. We can choose to steer our personal power toward integrity. The Devil reminds us that we are responsible for some of our shackles and that we're fully equipped to unchain ourselves. Liberation is far more expansive than the confinement of our comfortable excuses.

SUGGESTED EXERCISES

1. Research the importance of African and African American storytelling.

2. Watch "Honoring the Storytelling Tradition" by Open Road Media (1.5 min, captioned).

3. Read some Black folktales.

4. Check out AfroPoets.

5. Listen to the second season of the TMI Project's podcast, themed "Black Stories Matter."

Identifying as the Devil Card

How do you already embody the Devil card? Use this list of words commonly associated with this card to identify the qualities that you do and don't want to work with as you help create a radically more equitable world.

- Circle the qualities you already embody and can leverage as a superpower.

- Draw a heart around the qualities you want to embody more deeply or frequently.

- Draw a square around the qualities you want to transmute or avoid.

Free	Fear	Superficial	Illusions	Detachment
Obsession	Bondage	Makes excuses	Addiction	Shamelessness
Knows what they want	Smoke screens	Pleasure	Self-shaming	Dominates
Secret habits	Strong enough	Determined	Practical	Aware

Affirmations for Embodying the Devil Archetype

When confronting your deepest desires with the Devil, you might choose an affirmation to motivate you when the work is difficult. Affirmations can strengthen commitment by supporting your confidence in achieving personal and community goals. They can also help combat fear, anxiety, self-doubt, and loss of motivation, which are common feelings that come up in social justice work. You can chant them, write them down, meditate on them, add them to your phone background, or otherwise work with them consistently to keep focused on your objectives. Here are some examples.

"I always have options."

"I can start over anytime."

"I am neither superior nor inferior."

"Every day I make it easier to live in my integrity."

"Fear doesn't control me."

✎ Often, the most powerful affirmations are the ones we create for ourselves. Take some time to jot down your personal affirmations.

Magical Practices to Conjure the Devil Card

Quell infighting. Divest from spiritual capitalism. Do a harm audit of your organization. Examine the ways you hold power over other people. Make a list of how other people and forces hold power over you. Carry and distribute Narcan. Educate yourself about prison as modern-day slavery. Learn your rights. Support Black, queer BDSM spaces. Explore Mapping Police Violence. Identify your bad excuses. Challenge the licenses of abusive police officers. Offer community to isolated people. Rally against land privatization. Encourage loved ones to have more empathy for people of other races. Stop punishing yourself for what you did in the past. Learn to recognize normalized abuse. Boycott. Don't cross the picket line. Expose police brutality.

Becoming the Devil Archetype

Meditate on your relationship with the Devil, and use what you know to plan real-world action. By responding to these prompts, you are committing to doing the work—period.

SET A PERSONAL, RELATIONAL, OR COLLECTIVE INTENTION

✎ Name an objective that your work will center around.

✎ Plan specific actions for this objective that you will take as you embody the Devil card.

✎ This [day/week/month/event], I will embody the Devil card in my liberation work by _____

✎ This work is important because _____

✎ The affirmation I will repeat is _____

REFLECT ON YOUR EXPERIENCE

✎ Evolution is iterative and often nonlinear. As we pursue our goals, we must regularly evaluate our actions, mistakes, and learnings to inform the next cycles of change. Review your experience and identify what you can take with you as you move through your antiracism work.

- Successes
- Setbacks
- Frustrations
- Questions
- Other reflections
- Next steps

Combat Police Brutality

The Devil archetype conjures the topics of abuse through power—something we see within police forces around the world. Police brutality is an urgent and mortal issue. According to Mapping Police Violence, American police murdered 1,155 people in 2021, disproportionally people of color. There were only fifteen days that year when they did not kill anyone. Get familiar with the history of the American police force by learning its origins and how they led to modern abuses of power.

1. Define police brutality.

2. What is last year's racial breakdown of people hurt by police?

3. What is last year's racial breakdown of people killed by police?

4. Last year, what percent of police were charged and prosecuted for excessive force?

5. Last year, what percent of police were charged and prosecuted for murder?

6. What is the history of policing in America? Consider the Fugitive Slave Act of 1850, the Pinkerton agency, and watch patrols.

7. What does it mean to defund the police? What are the advantages? Disadvantages?

8. What does it mean to abolish the police? What are the advantages? Disadvantages?

9. What is victim blaming? List some real-life examples.

10. What is racial profiling?

11. What is "stop and frisk"?

12. What tools are police in your community using to prey on people of color?

13. What is qualified immunity? What steps can we take to end it?

16

THE TOWER

Do the best you can until you know better.
Then when you know better, do better.

—MAYA ANGELOU

Experiencing the Tower can mirror a butterfly's transformation. A cocooning caterpillar digests most of its tissues, turning into soup before freshly emerging as something radically different: a butterfly. It completely dissolves its old form, then leaves its protective home because it's time to grow. This is the path of the Tower: to leave structures where we no longer belong to expand into the spaciousness of who we're becoming. We do this for ourselves, our loved ones, and the planet. The materialistic Devil built the Tower from our expired habits, fears, and insecurities. Now that we've removed our chains, it's time to break out of the jailhouse. It might terrify you, but there's no going back.

The Tower asks one overarching question: do you want to return to the Devil's chains or would you prefer the Star's expansive potential and its restoration of hope? The answer is quite clear. Who wouldn't choose the Star? But in the dark night of the soul, it's tough to see the Star beyond the Tower, to even believe it exists. The fortress is in the way.

The turbulent Tower can represent chaos, upheaval, and massive paradigm shifts. When a bolt of lightning alerts us to the truth of the present moment, anything not built on a stable foundation will crumble. We can leave through the door, or we can go down with the ship. We can control ourselves, but not the fact that our house is burning down. Leaving home can be hard, but because you've changed, this is no longer your home. After removing the Devil's chains, we may feel overexposed, too vulnerable to leave the familiar. But we must let the Tower fall to prevent the temptation of returning to the Devil. We leave ourselves no choice but to head toward the distant Star and its healing waters.

The Tower doesn't always run on a scorched-earth platform. Yes, sometimes we need to destroy the whole thing—end a friendship, leave a job, change cities. Many foresters use fire to spark new tree growth. Other times we might only need to renovate a wing or replace the roof. Either way, the Tower meets us when we're ready to make a profound shift because our renewed future selves are waiting for us to show up. For now though, our focus is on surviving the present moment. Heavily fixating on the past makes way for depression; obsessive worry about the future creates anxiety. We just need to be here now, to sit and grieve our past selves. We may be ultimately grateful for our growth, but it is natural to have complicated feelings about the past. We witness the Tower's collapse because we choose to face our feelings instead of abandoning them. Our bodies and minds may be in chaos, but we hold faith that all nights eventually become mornings.

The Tower archetype can

- Make dramatic life changes, even when they're scary
- Gently navigate make-or-break moments
- Inspire people to radically shake the status quo
- Name the elephant in the room when no one else will
- Trust that things will get better
- Serve as a life coach, rescuer, housekeeper, or journalist

Embodied Keywords

Pull out the Tower card from one deck or several. Take a deep breath and pause. Gaze at the imagery. From a liberation perspective, envision yourself in the card's landscape. Be the archetype. Name some keywords that you personally associate with this card. Remember, your definitions are more relevant to your tarot reading than what's in the little white book. Here are a few keywords to help get you started.

Revelation, chaos, electricity, dissolution, repair, clarity, risk, discovery, free-falling, rage, major decisions, foundations, inevitability, humility, revolution, sober confrontation, anxiety, crisis, sudden change, honesty, insecurity, destroying to create, false premises, personal tests, anxiety, examining past trauma, liminal spaces, illusions, redefining protection, individuation

✎ **Your keywords:** _____

The Tower in Liberation Work

The Tower is here for revolution, whatever it takes.

Working with the Devil reveals the roots of our past addictions. The Tower rips them from the ground. Modeling this archetype in antiracism work can look like radically confronting oppressive structures and systems even when their necessary destruction seems impossible. These colossal fortresses loom large, but the Tower follows their gut to find opportunities to help dismantle the machine. This work is both external and internal.

Tower moments include the crisis of realization and the responsibility of repair. The Devil disclosed certain truths, so ignorance is now a less viable excuse. We know better, so we must do better. To demolish the Tower is to reveal the immensity of our potential for true metamorphosis. We can always become more effective liberators. We just need to trust in a future we cannot easily see.

Tower experiences transform us through healthy, generative chaos. A Tower's destruction is a chance to step back, plainly see who we've become, and decide how to reinvent the way we show up as an activist. How can you apply your expanded knowledge and resilience to protect and elevate people with less privilege? How will you use your "identity upgrades" to cultivate community solidarity? Consider whether your activism

- Addresses your inherent racism (regardless of race)
- Jeopardizes your comfort or safety
- Costs relationships with friends, family, or other groups
- Takes time away from more leisurely pastimes
- Disrupts predominantly white spaces

- Shows up, even when no one is looking
- Is consistent, despite trends in news cycles
- Truly feels like becoming less privileged
- Challenges family values from childhood
- Is ever performative

Realizing that we have much more still to do after doing so much can feel crushing, especially when we're tired. But the assumption that any of us have done all we can is an illusion framed by the Tower's shadows. Many of us are still, albeit often without choice, active participants in racist societies. The Tower reflects our choices to evolve despite struggle, not our attempts to become perfect activists. Rome didn't fall in a day. When we're acutely shocked by how we still perpetuate racism, we refuse to let it deflate our commitment. May the Tower's rubble remind us that all edifices are built incrementally from smaller parts. Everyone occasionally feels discouraged and far from achieving their goals. But the dark night of the soul is just that—a night. A new morning will come. It arrives faster when we work through difficult feelings instead of pretending they don't exist. The Tower has fallen and we can't hide from ourselves anymore.

Correspondences for Inspiration

Consider exploring sources of inspiration that you connect with the Tower card. To help get you started, here are a few popular associations.

Moon conjunct Mars, iron, garnet, bloodstone, lodestone, jasper, wolves, bears, vultures, all stinging insects, horseradish, garlic, rue, pepper, chili, capers, leeks, radish, nettle, chestnut, pennyroyal, cyprus, agarwood, dragon's blood, odiferous woods

✎ What reminds you of the Tower card? How do these things inspire you to keep going?

How the Tower Card Can Show Up

There are as many interpretations of tarot as there are people who have ever lived. There is no completely universal card interpretation because there is no completely universal perspective on life. Your and your clients' interpretations are what matter the most during a reading. Of all the possible magical ingredients, we humans are the most powerful in enacting real-world change. However, there are strong collective energies around the themes that appear more frequently when a particular archetype shows up. Here are some of those common motifs.

THE BALANCED TOWER ARCHETYPE

- Realizes when they need to be the catalyst
- Admits when they are wrong
- Finds comfort in the void, rather than despair
- Lives in the present moment
- Wants to heal
- Isn't bound by comfort
- Cuts negative ties for good

✎ **My relationship to the Tower archetype feels balanced when** _____

THE IMBALANCED TOWER ARCHETYPE

- Doesn't let go easily
- Avoids change
- Entertains drama
- Justifies harmful behavior
- Seeks shortcuts to healing
- Doesn't believe in a better future
- Believes the system's tools are the only method to disassemble it

✎ **My relationship to the Tower archetype feels imbalanced when** _____

Moving Beyond Allyship

After moving past, integrating, or otherwise transforming our devils, we've unblocked ourselves from demolishing or repairing the Tower. The fortress provides safety and refuge, but is familiar enough to tempt us into reverting to the Devil. A close look at the Tower exposes its cracks and falling hinges. We tell ourselves it's easier to stay than go into the wilderness with no compass but a mysterious and faint glow in the distance. The Tower doesn't quite feel right, but it's comfortable. We decide it's good enough.

One day lightning suddenly strikes the building and our hearts sink. We instantly remember the Tower's disrepair, then start to hear it crumble. Still, the prospect of leaving is frightening. We've made so much progress and even found a place to stay—departure feels daunting. The idea is so unsettling that we get into bed, close our eyes, and try to convince ourselves the Tower will be fine. When crumbling grows louder, we resign to what our intuition has told us since we arrived: we don't belong here. Leaving was once a choice, but now it's our only option.

Intuition first whispers to us. Repeatedly ignoring the inner voice only raises the volume until it's shouting at us. The amount of time we wait to listen is often indirectly proportional to the number of choices available. When we disregard our intuition, we put ourselves in the position of having to jump out of the Tower. Had we listened to the first summons, we could have planned our transition away from the Tower. Had we listened, we could have simply exited through the front door.

Tower card experiences teach us that transformation, whether chosen or forced, is a nonnegotiable part of the journey. You don't get to level up without changing *something*. When we dust ourselves off and return to our antiracism work, we may start with baby steps. Such small steps allow us to ease into realistic and highly sustainable habits, preventing early overwhelm and burnout. Transitional fatigue can lead us to romanticize relapsing into the Devil's jailhouse because it's easier than enduring the discomfort of transformation. So we take those baby steps. Small steps forward build confidence and momentum more than taking five steps forward and ten steps back. One foot in front of the other, we travel deeper and deeper into our antiracism work. But we can't stop at baby steps. They're launching pads, not destinations.

At some point, allyship must go beyond small gestures. We must energetically exit the Tower after we peer out of a window, gaze at a wide expanse, and realize the potential for racial healing beyond this familiar structure. Temperance told us that we're the alchemists of our lives. Our devotion to a more equitable future requires experimentation to reveal how our contributions could be more potent and effective. The Tower's demise is inevitable. Will the disturbance discourage you or inspire you to show up to your work with renewed commitment? You get to choose.

Keep in mind, our spheres of influence are always bigger than we think. We've grown so much in the journey so far, but our evolution isn't just for us. Our work is urgent; lives are at stake. The future needs who we've become. So does the present. It's not enough to be an ally anymore. You know enough to make deeper commitments in the fight against systemic racism. In *How to Be an Antiracist*, Ibram X. Kendi says, "The opposite of racist isn't 'not racist,' it is anti-racist." Then he defines both terms:

> **Racist**: *One who is supporting a racist policy through their actions of inaction or expressing a racist idea*

> **Antiracist**: *One who is supporting an antiracist policy through their actions or expressing an antiracist idea*

Not racist may mean "supporting racist policies through their actions of inaction"—is this you? How so?

Being an ally isn't the endgame. Allyship is important, but it's foundational. Allyship is just a starting point. If we stay there, our passion atrophies, and going through the motions of being a "good ally" eventually has the same impact as doing nothing at all. Supporting a cause is nice, but actively working for it is better. It's not enough to say you support racial equity. How do you continually show and expand your support? What risks are you taking? What indicates a need to leap from the Tower's deceptive protection?

We've got to move past baby steps. We've got to go further. We've got to become coconspirators.

Legal associate Violet Rush describes what it means for white people to be coconspirators:

To be a white co-conspirator means to deliberately acknowledge that people of color are criminalized for dismantling white supremacy. It means we choose to take on the consequences of participating in a criminalized act, and we choose to support and center people of color in the reproductive justice movement.... Oftentimes when white people are exposed to the term co-conspirator, they assume that it is in relation to criminal law; for example, a co-conspirator in a crime. However, the issue of conspiracy is often less emotionally burdensome for white students because conspiracy implies separation from direct harm caused to others.

Supporting a conspiracy isn't the same thing as actively taking part in it. Initial allyship is a common first step. Learning gives us greater responsibility to act on our knowledge. At this point in the Major Arcana, we've learned enough to become more active participants in the racial equity movement.

When the Tower falls, there's no going back. Uneasiness during transitions is alchemical; addressing and working through that anxiety strengthen us. You may have plenty of tools in your arsenal, but make sure to add more courage. This card asks: how can you become a more useful warrior in fighting for and protecting people of color? The urgency of racial equity begs us to go harder.

Dante Barry, executive director of the Million Hoodies Movement for Justice, says, "Black folks are readily risking their lives every day purely by existing," while many white allies are overly worried about their uncomfortable feelings. You can be an activist while processing difficult emotions. We all are. If you are white and your primary concern is your emotional distress, think back to the Magician and revisit your reasons for being here. The comparison between your feelings and your intentions can be a reminder that Black lives matter more than your guilt, fear, or refusal to intensify your social justice efforts.

Join the conspiracy. The conspiracy? Genuine inclusion and equity. Let the Tower fall. This time we listen to our intuition and head toward the distant glow that calls us by name.

SUGGESTED EXERCISES

1. Watch Ava DuVernay's documentary *13th* (full feature, 1 h 40 min, captioned).

2. Read "Explaining White Privilege to a Broke White Person" by Gina Crosley-Corcoran.

3. Send a Letter for Black Lives to someone you know, and prepare to discuss using the website's forty-page conversation guide.

4. Listen to Earwolf's *What Did We Learn?* with Alicia Garza and Wyatt Cenac.

5. Read "What Abolitionists Do" by Dan Berger, Mariame Kaba, and David Stein.

6. Listen to Amanda Seales's "Side Effects of White Women" episode of *Small Doses: Potent Truths for Everyday Use.*

Identifying as the Tower Card

How do you already embody the Tower card? Use this list of words commonly associated with this card to identify the qualities that you do and don't want to work with as you help create a radically more equitable world.

- Circle the qualities you already embody and can leverage as a superpower.

- Draw a heart around the qualities you want to embody more deeply or frequently.

- Draw a square around the qualities you want to transmute or avoid.

Ready for freedom	Overwhelmed	Illusion	Inspired	Uncompromising
Awakening	Owns one's volition	Flexible to change	Radical honesty	Security
Fearful	Avoidant	Rigid self-perception	Escapism	Lives in the present moment
Discomfort	Darkness	Trauma	Misunderstanding	Prioritizes comfort

Affirmations for Embodying the Tower Archetype

As you move beyond the Tower's shadow, you might choose an affirmation to motivate you when the work is difficult. Affirmations can strengthen commitment by supporting your confidence in achieving personal and community goals. They can also help combat fear, anxiety, self-doubt, and loss of motivation, which are common feelings that come up in social justice work. You can chant them, write them down, meditate on them, add them to your phone background, or otherwise work with them consistently to keep focused on your objectives. Here are some examples.

"I can go back to the Devil, or I can transform into the Star."

"I don't need to see the future to believe in it."

"I create tomorrow with yesterday's ashes."

"This is supposed to be uncomfortable."

"There's no going back."

 Often, the most powerful affirmations are the ones we create for ourselves. Take some time to jot down your personal affirmations.

Magical Practices to Conjure the Tower Card

Challenge perceptions of what an activist looks like. Identify how fear controls your organization's plans and efforts. Confront your or others' white guilt. Sacrifice one thing every week for the greater good. Take social risks. Remove racist monuments. Rename community institutions named after tyrants. Occupy buildings. Disrupt harmful journalism. Remove hierarchy from your organization's structure. Address optical allyship. Give healthy ultimatums. Stop doing it "the way you've always done it." Use your body to protect others'. Create autonomous systems of mutual aid. Allow yourself to be publicly humbled.

Becoming the Tower Archetype

Meditate on your relationship with the Tower and use what you know to plan real-world action. By responding to these prompts, you are committing to doing the work—period.

SET A PERSONAL, RELATIONAL, OR COLLECTIVE INTENTION

✎ Name an objective that your work will center around.

✎ Plan specific actions for this objective that you will take as you embody the Tower card.

✎ This [day/week/month/event], I will embody the Tower card in my liberation work by _____

✎ This work is important because _____

✎ The affirmation I will repeat is _____

REFLECT ON YOUR EXPERIENCE

✎ Evolution is iterative and often nonlinear. As we pursue our goals, we must regularly evaluate our actions, mistakes, and learnings to inform the next cycles of change. Review your experience and identify what you can take with you as you move through your antiracism work.

- Successes

- Setbacks

- Frustrations

- Questions

- Other reflections

- Next steps

Understand Prison Systems

The Tower speaks to internal fortresses, but also literal ones. The American prison system is modern-day slavery wrapped in different packaging. It's a monolith obscuring our ability to envision a world without racial oppression. It's no surprise that this institution disproportionately imprisons Black people. Like how the Tower confronts uncomfortable truths, confront the realities of American imprisonment and the many ways the system prohibits our collective freedom.

1. Define "prison industrial complex."

2. List the percentages of people incarcerated in ten countries. Then find the percentage of Black men who are incarcerated in the U.S. What do these numbers tell you?

3. Describe the following types of prison systems:

> Juvenile
>
> Local
>
> State
>
> Federal
>
> Immigration
>
> Territorial
>
> Public
>
> Private

4. Make a chart of the racial demographics in the U.S. prison system.

5. List ten businesses that profit from the prison system.

6. Describe how prison shows up as modern-day slavery.

7. Describe the cash bail system, including its purpose and consequences.

8. Describe mandatory sentencing, including its purpose and consequences.

9. Describe the 1994 crime bill, formally titled the Violent Crime Control and Law Enforcement Act, and its impact.

10. Name ways that formerly incarcerated people are supported in reintegrating into your community. How can you aid these efforts?

11. Familiarize yourself with prison reform movements and decide whether the new systems are progressive or dangerous. Explain your reasoning.

12. Name and plan to interact with five resources, such as books, organizations, or websites, you can use to understand the criminal justice system.

17

THE STAR

*You can't separate peace from freedom because no one can be at
peace unless [they have their] freedom.*

—MALCOLM X

The Star rises from the Tower's ashes, shamelessly radiating their inner star power with brilliant vulnerability. They have made it through the dark night of the soul, and now they're ready to do the crucial work of healing, the work of rebuilding our interior landscapes and our external surroundings. This card is the emerging sunshine and crisp air after a storm. After the Tower's destruction, there's nothing blocking the reality that we are full of potential fueled by passion and moderated by rest. Our past biases and adverse behaviors no longer obscure our innate shine. We are free to model an archetype that dutifully follows their north star while writing a new story for themselves. Yes, we get to rewrite our stories. The Star, free of defenses, is possibility embodied.

The Star is a reminder that we are on the right path, even if the road is dimly lit. This is an archetype of trust, faith, rejuvenation, bright prospects, hope, ritual, healing, and time. Here, starlight illuminates the way. While faint compared to moonlight and sunlight, the Star provides just enough brightness to follow our inner guiding light. The Star isn't focused on rapid evolution, but rather flow. Key seventeen reduces to eight, the Strength card. Together, these cards tell us that choosing to heal is inherently courageous and creative. It takes nerve and imagination to cultivate new worlds. At the Star, we integrate what we've learned thus far through streams that generously flow our interactions with ourselves, our loved ones, and the greater collective. This archetype rests and revives their belief in the future, rejuvenating their motivation. They witness the endurance of the stars in the sky and hope their efforts help social progress for generations. The Star never withholds their brilliance when opportunities arise. They are generous with their starlight because they truly believe in a more luminous future.

The Star can

- Deliver deeper meaning and purpose
- Know their current true purpose
- Exhibit renewed self-esteem
- Show generosity in unique ways
- Use creativity to heal
- Expand their perspectives regularly
- Serve as an entertainer, technology worker, researcher, or event planner

Embodied Keywords

Pull out the Star card from one deck or several. Take a deep breath and pause. Gaze at the imagery. From a liberation perspective, envision yourself in the card's landscape. Be the archetype. Name some keywords that you personally associate with this card. Remember, your definitions are more relevant to your tarot reading than what's in the little white book. Here are a few keywords to help get you started.

Renewal, hope, spirituality, flow, confidence, vulnerability, rest, dreaming, inspiration, balance, belief, relaxation, visibility, interconnectedness, awe, imagination, honesty, guidance, soul retrieval, good omens, assistance, promise, open channels, buoyancy, peace, germination, mental vitality, exploration

✎ Your keywords: _____

The Star in Liberation Work

The inventive Star is the courageous healer, recompensing for their and their ancestors' wrongs while forging new trails under the new moon. Their work remains challenging, but their sincere confidence in a more ideal future makes it easier to focus on their north star. Their hope is renewed, and their vision gets clearer every day. Acting with faith, they serve as luminaries to their peers, inspiring them to believe in a mission enough to challenge their own hang-ups. The Star knows they'll never be who they were before the Tower. They are the latest version of themselves and must use their updated operating system to navigate antiracism work. Even though it might take some time to get used to it, they faithfully push forward. They don't wait for the sun. If they must sketch tomorrow's picture in darkroom lighting, they will. Nothing can dampen their conviction.

The Star's definition of healing extends far beyond their personal selves, as they remain mindful of collective trauma and its impact on their community. They recognize that both human misconduct (e.g., genocide) and natural disasters (e.g., floods) can leave significant effects on victims' physical, social, mental, and emotional health, especially when they happen to underserved people. The Star as healer turns their own and others' lenses toward collective healing: admitting the reality of the situation, confessing how they've perpetuated oppression, then demonstrating accountability by repairing damage and restoring access to resources. The Star is a vehicle for restorative justice. They value personal healing, but *really* care about community healing.

The Star appreciates that everything is interconnected. They cultivate networks of peer support and mutual aid. They act with flow, but with urgency. Procrastinating community healing is a dangerous privilege that risks the construction of new towers. Remedying existing structures isn't enough, so the Star leverages rebellious vision and radical hope to help cultivate a society free of brutality, competition, individualism, cruelty, and subjugation. They may never know enough to feel completely comfortable in their activism, but their north star keeps them going. Awkward feelings don't justify self-imposed roadblocks. The Star paves new avenues of collective care that bring communities together. They watch children so caregivers can rest. They make enough dinner to share with their neighbors. They arrange car pools to sit-ins and install community fridges. They plan block parties. They share job leads with people struggling to pay rising rent costs. They set up mutual aid funds. They cultivate accessible spaces for community gatherings. The Star's inclusive definition of community helps curb the modern epidemic of loneliness. What good is starlight if we never share it?

Correspondences for Inspiration

Consider exploring sources of inspiration that you associate with the Star card. To help get you started, here are a few popular correspondences.

> Aquarius, Saturn as liberator, galbanum, euphorbium, otters, peacocks, chalcedony, amethyst, crystal, turquoise, quartz, olive, fir, moss, skullcap, fruit trees, dragon lilies, flowing water, vessels, stardust

✎ **What reminds you of the Star card? How do these things inspire you to keep going?**

How the Star Card Can Show Up

There are as many interpretations of tarot as there are people who have ever lived. There is no completely universal card interpretation because there is no completely universal perspective on life. Your and your clients' interpretations are what matter the most during a reading. Of all the possible magical ingredients, we humans are the most powerful in enacting real-world change. However, there are strong collective energies around the themes that appear more frequently when a particular archetype shows up. Here are some of those common motifs.

THE BALANCED STAR

- Inspires raw honesty
- Conjures hope
- Experiences awe in the mundane
- Shares their light
- Dares to dream bigger
- Goes with the flow, but holds on to truth
- Renews devotion to their mission

✎ **My relationship to the Star archetype feels balanced when** _____

THE IMBALANCED STAR

- Overthinks
- Acknowledges harm, but avoids responsibility
- Discourages others
- Hoards out of fear of the unknown
- Disengages
- Loses faith in their causes
- Is bored

✎ My relationship to the Star archetype feels imbalanced when _____

Cultivating Rest in Your Community

When we turn toward the Star, we might choose to revisit the Mizuta Masahide haiku, "Barn's burnt down—now I can see the moon." We can also see the stars. Albeit dimmer than sunlight or moonlight, their radiance lights our way. It is dark and we are vulnerable, but the glimmer of distant suns hints that we are secure to rest and head onward.

After the Tower's trials expose our raw selves (1 + 6 = 7, a key that can represent individuation), we're safe to come home to ourselves, to exchange our defenses for grace, rest, and healing. Because 18 reduces to 9 and 9 is adjacent to 10, the Star can indicate our proximity to the end of this phase of our lifelong antiracist activism. But we don't need to rush if we're feeling post-Tower burnout. The Star treasures rest and relaxes when genuine fatigue impedes their work. Our ability to thrive depends on our willingness to rest.

It can be exhausting to exist as a person of color in an inherently racist society. White aggression and violence can happen in nearly any public space, even the grocery store. Stories about victims like Breonna Taylor remind us that home is not guaranteed to be a completely safe space. Our phones aren't necessarily safe either, as stories about surveillance abuse become more frequent.

Many acknowledge that people of color deserve equitable access to resources that promote prosperity. However, some people overlook the need for dedicated time and space to repair physically, mentally, and energetically.

Consider "sleep gaps." Compared to white Americans, Black Americans are five times more likely to get less than six hours of sleep a night and feel tired during the day. The Sleep Foundation reports similar, yet less dramatic, disparities for nonwhite people overall. They note:

> A growing body of evidence points to sleeping problems as an area of significant health disparities between racial and ethnic groups. Because of sleep's critical role in overall wellness, sleep insufficiency may help explain other health disparities, such as the higher rates of cardiovascular disease among people of color.

Considering the United States's cultural and financial influence, it wouldn't be surprising to find similar disparities between the dominant race and those they hold power over. Structural oppression's assault on marginalized communities' rest isn't new. For instance, Benjamin Reiss wrote in the *LA Times*:

> The racial sleep gap is largely a matter of unequal access to safe, reliable and comfortable sleep environments, and this sleeping inequality has a long history. For centuries, whites have tacitly accepted—and even actively created—such inequality. Aboard the ships of the transatlantic slave trade, African captives were made to sleep en masse in the hold, often while chained together. Once in the New World, enslaved people were usually still made to sleep in tight quarters, sometimes on the bare floor, and they struggled to snatch any sleep at all while chained together in the coffle. Slaveholders systematically disallowed privacy as they attempted round-the-clock surveillance, and enslaved women were especially susceptible at night to sexual assault from white men.

Rest deprivation is a white supremacist tool. Rising living costs require more labor, reducing available time, energy, and attention for organizing against systems of oppression. Wage slavery frequently precludes revolutionary rest. And wage slavery frequently precludes revolution. In "Reparations for Black People Should Include Rest," Janine Francois explains:

> Just as sleep deprivation was used as a means to control slaves, the modern-day sleep gap continues to weigh down many Black people, like me, today. I can feel it in me: It breaks my spirit, as I exist in between half-conscious states; never fully awake or asleep, never able to distinguish between the two. This may be the true power of racism—its force encompasses everything, seeping into our dreams at night and deflating our capacity to envision a better future. How can the radical Black imagination

rebel against a system that so thoroughly seeks to destroy us? What would a future look like where we are liberated, reparations are paid, and we can finally rest?

Rest liberation won't just look like more paid time off or nail salon gift cards for jobs well done. Remember, the Star doesn't attach their value to their productivity. They pride themselves on making space. Rest makes space for growth, enjoyment, and relaxation. We can't thrive if we're too tired to try.

Rest liberation requires consistent integration of rest for marginalized people. No white person has a greater right to rest than anyone else.

Oppression and trauma have long inhibited many Black people from opportunities to do nothing and explore the imaginative creativity that comes from doing nothing, sleeping well, and relaxing. Embodying the Star, we don't just expand equity within existing structures. The new world requires new systems of collective care. Many full-time jobs don't pay enough for independent living. Globally, government aid is often barely, if even, enough to survive. The Star doesn't stop caring after someone sprouts. They want to see them blossom. Cultivating rest for marginalized people is collective liberation, is justice, is reparations. The Star says so.

SUGGESTED EXERCISES

1. Check out the Nap Ministry and learn about their purpose. Consider how their work may inspire your actions in your own community.

2. Buy or borrow a copy of *Black Imagination*, curated by Natasha Marin.

3. Envision what reparations that include rest would look like.

4. Create a list of five ways you can offer rest to BIPOC in your community. Perform those actions and add onto the list as you think of or learn about additional things you can do. For example, you might offer to watch someone's child so they can take a nap or an evening to themselves.

5. If you have the means, send money to BIPOC to help create more leisure in their lives.

Identifying as the Star Card

How do you already embody the Star card? Use this list of words commonly associated with this card to identify the qualities that you do and don't want to work with as you help create a radically more equitable world.

- Circle the qualities you already embody and can leverage as a superpower.
- Draw a heart around the qualities you want to embody more deeply or frequently.
- Draw a square around the qualities you want to transmute or avoid.

Inspired	Renewed	Vulnerable	Dreaming	Defensive
Ready for new narratives	Wide perception	Hopeful	Rigid	Isolation
Overthinking	Generous with talents	Fantastical thinking	Cluttered mind	Visionary
Rebelliousness	Faith	Insightful	Afraid to heal	Confident

Affirmations for Embodying the Star Archetype

As you rejuvenate with the Star, you might choose an affirmation to motivate you when the work is difficult. Affirmations can strengthen commitment by supporting your confidence in achieving personal and community goals. They can also help combat fear, anxiety, self-doubt, and loss of motivation, which are common feelings that come up in social justice work. You can chant them, write them down, meditate on them, add them to your phone background, or otherwise work with them consistently to keep focused on your objectives. Here are some examples.

"My healing helps heal the world."

"I'm ready to step into my light."

"Every day I renew my motivation."

"My future self appreciates what I'm doing today."

"May ease flow through me and unto others."

✎ Often, the most powerful affirmations are the ones we create for ourselves. Take some time to jot down your personal affirmations.

Magical Practices to Conjure the Star Card

Create programs for marginalized youth to follow their dreams. Increase access to therapy, where culturally relevant. Donate paid time off to a Black colleague. Support radical street artists. Fund mobile showers and laundromats. Rejuvenate organizational morale. Model integrity for your peers. Start a group of people who take turns watching each other's children. Open spaces where people can nap when shelters are closed during the day. Get to know your neighbors. Help update your organization's mission statement. Write a list of simple ways to renew your motivation daily. Defend public access to clean water.

Becoming the Star Archetype

Meditate on your relationship with the Star, and use what you know to plan real-world action. By responding to these prompts, you are committing to doing the work—period.

SET A PERSONAL, RELATIONAL, OR COLLECTIVE INTENTION

✎ Name an objective that your work will center around.

✎ Plan specific actions for this objective that you will take as you embody the Star card.

✎ This [day/week/month/event], I will embody the Star card in my liberation work by _____

✎ This work is important because _____

✎ The affirmation I will repeat is _____

REFLECT ON YOUR EXPERIENCE

✎ Evolution is iterative and often nonlinear. As we pursue our goals, we must regularly evaluate our actions, mistakes, and learnings to inform the next cycles of change. Review your experience and identify what you can take with you as you move through your antiracism work.

- Successes
- Setbacks
- Frustrations
- Questions
- Other reflections
- Next steps

BUILDING A TOOLKIT

Know Your Local Schools

The Star represents radical belief in the future. Today's youth lead tomorrow's world; thus liberation work should consider schools and mass indoctrination through white supremacist curriculums. After completing the following prompts, choose an action to take for local children at the margins.

1. What does your public school system's antiracism mission and strategy look like? Are their antiracist goals specific, measurable, actionable, relevant, and time-bound?

2. Define the roles and responsibilities of a teacher.

3. How is antiracism embedded in local curriculums?

4. What is the 1619 Project and why does it exist? How does the project relate to what you learned in grade school?

5. List five examples of grade schools taking antiracist action. Name their initiatives and impact thus far.

6. Know the root. How are your local public schools funded?

7. What are the racial demographics of teachers within your nearest elementary, middle, and high schools?

8. What is the role of a school counselor? Why do they exist, what are their responsibilities, and what's within their range of power?

9. What is the role of a school resource officer? Why do they exist, what are their responsibilities, and what's within their range of power?

10. Does your school system have a contract with the local police department?

11. Describe the school-to-prison pipeline.

12. The 2011 report "Breaking Schools' Rules: A Statewide Study on How School Discipline Relates to Students' Success and Juvenile Justice Involvement" by the CSJ Justice Center exposed that children suspended or expelled for discretionary violations are nearly three times more likely to be in contact with the juvenile justice system within the next year. Read recent stories and statistics. How often are Black students suspended or expelled today? How have the numbers changed since 2011? Why do you think they've changed? What percentage of these children have educational disabilities? What might this connection convey?

18

THE MOON

... momma
help me
turn the face of history
to your face.
—JUNE JORDAN

The last "night card" of the Major Arcana, the Moon returns to the interior. Our days begin at night, moonlight waning as we anticipate the sunrise. Key eighteen combines Mars (1)'s electrifying energy with Saturn (8)'s trials and dedication to result in the number nine, suggesting a nearby sense of fulfillment as the result of all the energy we've embodied so far in our Major Arcana adventure. Here, we're still recovering from the Tower. The Star initiates healing, and the Moon takes it further when they call us to sit with the confusion that can arise after we've undergone a major transformation. The Moon affectionally investigates their inner multitudes to confront their fears and continue healing. Working with the Moon helps us cultivate inner resiliency that withstands any doubts or setbacks that become visible underneath full sunlight. We deserve the Sun card's levity, but we must retreat and check in with our interior before risking exposure. When tempted to jump from the rejuvenated Star to our jovial Sun, we can't forget: sunshine burns without proper preparation and protection.

Lying beneath the Sun's rays is alluring—simultaneous relaxation, ease, and glee. However, we rob ourselves of solar ecstasy when we cut to key nineteen without deeply tuning our intuition. We have changed undoubtedly and immeasurably. We need the fullness of the Moon to reveal what that signifies for our inner selves before we return to the outer world. Jumping to the Sun on the

Fool's journey is like playing a favorite movie on standard definition: it's *okay*, but it's tough to thoroughly understand the movie without seeing everything we want—or need—to see to understand the film. Without audio description, we may settle to follow the movie at a surface level. Before the Sun card, we must gaze within to clearly and vividly witness the Sun's radiance and the glory of the planet that it powers.

The Moon provides additional light for the Fool's journey, but it's still not enough for full vision at night. They must rely heavily on their intuition. Even though they can only see a few feet ahead of them, they take note of symbols that provoke memories, dreamscapes, feelings, divine messages, and instincts. Beyond strictly linear thinking, they plunge into inner depths to explore the cosmos within, where there are no right angles. The Moon intuitively strings together life's events and phases to understand how and why they've changed. This practice is often confusing yet essential.

At times, internally processing external events bewilders the Moon. They arrange memories and timelines to create mental narratives of assorted experiences. The distance between their embodied experiences and their new interpretations can be wide. Struggling to reconcile this disharmony may tempt the Moon to gaslight themselves, wondering "Which story is more accurate?" and "What story elements are actually projections?" Each account may include nearly accurate information, but it's impossible to totally detach from subconscious influence. Neither story is "right." With this understanding, the Moon surveys their plotlines, seeking moments that heighten their intuition. They translate the data into knowledge, revealing deeply embedded subconscious needs, desires, motivations, and fears. Their revelations help secure their sense of self and autonomy before the outer world tries to define who they are. The Moon archetype emerges from uncharted ocean cliffs—bringing wisdom from nonlinear information, synchronicities, cycles, recurring life themes, ancestral wisdom, primal instinct, and dreams—more enlightened. They approach the Sun with a stabler sense of who they are, where they are, and what it all could mean.

This archetype reminds us that every one of our ancestors lived under the same moon. For most of recorded history, people have relied on lunar cycles for time tracking, agricultural planning and predictions, conjugation, and even collecting taxes. All six inhabited continents have long histories of following our dear satellite. The Moon channels their ancestral past for inspiration, comfort, companionship, and healing. They make magic when they break generational patterns of harm, within and outside of the family.

The Moon archetype can

- Spot illusions
- Trust their gut instincts easily
- Be receptive
- Appear mysterious
- Read people well
- Analyze dreams and nightmares
- Sustain commitment to healing
- Serve as a trauma-informed practitioner, cat rescue volunteer, sex worker, fisher, or park ranger

Embodied Keywords

Pull out the Moon card from one deck or several. Take a deep breath and pause. Gaze at the imagery. From a liberation perspective, envision yourself in the card's landscape. Be the archetype. Name some keywords that you personally associate with this card. Remember, your definitions are more relevant to your tarot reading than what's in the little white book. Here are a few keywords to help get you started.

Subconscious, intuition, fear, illusion, release, cycles, insecurity, dreamwork, mystery, psychic, receptivity, shadows, deep memories, ancestry (blood or otherwise), nonlinearity, primal nature, storytelling, visions, spirituality, fluidity, emotions, healing, timing, lunar living, inner truth, spirals, self-discovery without rules

Your keywords: _____

The Moon in Liberation Work

The Moon soberly faces historical realities and exposes how deeply they impact us today. The Moon sits below Justice in the three-line Major Arcana grid, with Justice reinforcing the need to reveal obscured information for fair evaluation. The Emperor hovers over Justice, demanding we preserve, protect, and publicize evidence of abuse, invasion, and subjugation. Remembering our oppressive past is key to today's work of building the future.

Among other motives, oppressors use historical erasure to revise, deny, and bury stories of harm against marginalized people. They also obscure testimonies of joy, celebration, and pride. Without the connective tissue of shared history, the sense of collective belonging can wane as generations come and go. Abusers suppress the past to disconnect people, foster apathy, and watch our stories, traditions, and languages fade into oblivion. Cultural erasure can be a long, gradual process, but the clandestine strategy of splintering a community that sets the scene for coerced and forced assimilation into how oppressors do—and don't want—to include them in wider society.

The Emperor-Justice-Moon column instructs us to use any available light to illuminate hidden truths for the sake of a more just society. We excavate, rest, and repeat. When discovering things we don't want to know or accept, we may sense rising anxiety. Some treat anxiety pangs like alerts that signal particularly deep states of reflection. Others take them as a sign to drink water and go to bed. No one can dictate how you navigate your subconscious. There are no completely universal rules about intuition. We might use it to enter the interior, examine inner narratives and personal truths, and exit trance states. We could also use it to choose hiking routes and order from restaurants. There's never only one path to liberation.

Our partnership with the Moon card can be incredibly personal, but we make the most out of it when we experiment with our discoveries in the outside world. However, beware. We might believe our ego when we lie to ourselves, but routinely exercising intuition makes it nearly impossible to ignore the realities we hide from ourselves. Pretending that lynching ended after the 1920s, barring Black history from public schools, reviving massive book bans—every fact, story, and object forbidden by white supremacist culture shows us who our oppressors are, how they think, and what they fear about people of color.

The Moon watches over and protects femmes, especially those at the margin. The Moon witnesses them when the patriarchy will not. Current and historical communities associate the moon with menstrual cycles—the moon usually undergoes thirteen cycles a year and so do many women, who bleed roughly every twenty-eight days. Since ancient times, generations of moongazers across cultures have regarded the moon as the celestial femme—the elegant, the trickster, the whore, the mother, a holy extraterrestrial witness. In contrast, white-dominant, patriarchal societies that associate the moon with womanhood tend to disparage our nearest heavenly neighbor. Their disrespect of women and persistent dependence on linear thinking paint the moon and its spiral dance as the "Other." (We can try to imagine the backgrounds of the people who thought it was a good idea to leave 400,000 pounds of trash, equipment, and human waste on the moon.)

In some places, broader spectrums and increased representation have given comfort to people who finally feel safe to unveil their authentic identities to other people. Cultures of white domination often illustrate the WASP cishet man as the default representation of a human being. When a civilization's social acceptance standards are limited, even more of us get labeled "other." The moon as other guards the disenfranchised, the poor, the disabled, the forgotten, as well as the queer, trans, and nonbinary. To embody the moon is to develop community amongst weirdos incrementally and cyclically. Through sincerity, consistency, and vulnerable eccentricity, the freedom to be ourselves with our chosen family elicits aspects we've buried out of shame, ridicule, fear of exclusion, or other threats to our emotional, physical, mental, and spiritual safety. Letting loose with other outcasts can help build confidence and psychological resilience in public arenas.

The moon shines more brightly upon people whose divergence from "normal" has upset, shocked, or disgusted passersby into refusing to look at them again. They pretend we're invisible, figures in the dark underbelly of humankind. But they don't know we have the moon, nor are they aware that it evokes even more reasons to love ourselves from the inside out. Together we gaze at the moon and let our freak flag fly. The power of community care and affection intimidates our invisibility. We are prouder than we were yesterday. When the sun rises tomorrow, they won't be able to miss us.

Correspondences for Inspiration

Consider exploring sources of inspiration that you connect with the Moon card. To help get you started, here are a few popular associations.

> Fossils, motherwort, red storax, pearl, coral, moonstone, selenite, amethyst, shellfish, dog, wolf, fish, owls, fig, hazel, willow, lilies, datura, jasmine, bodies of water, clocks, journals, spirals

✎ What reminds you of the Moon card? How do these things inspire you to keep going?

How the Moon Card Can Show Up

There are as many interpretations of tarot as there are people who have ever lived. There is no completely universal card interpretation because there is no completely universal perspective on life. Your and your clients' interpretations are what matter the most during a reading. Of all the possible magical ingredients, we humans are the most powerful in enacting real-world change. However, there are strong collective energies around the themes that appear more frequently when a particular archetype shows up. Here are some of those common motifs.

THE BALANCED MOON

- Is in touch with their natural self
- Approaches confusion with patience
- Gives their ancestors a voice
- Romances the mystery
- Commits to deep healing
- Has a complex view of themselves
- Takes cyclical approaches

✎ My relationship to the Moon archetype feels balanced when _____

THE IMBALANCED MOON

- Disregards deeper emotional issues
- Lies to themselves
- Is disconnected from reality
- Doesn't have a sense of self
- Can't find safe spaces
- Ignores natural cycles
- Denies their inner wildness

✎ My relationship to the Moon archetype feels imbalanced when _____

The Moon Says Rewilding Is a Natural Right

The darkness at the turn of a new day can bring healing, fear, or something in between. Here we reach the parts of ourselves that the sun's rays can't reach. Out in the open, rings of tree stumps remind us of our inner complexity. When we accept that our innermost selves are our wildest selves, we stimulate embodied healing.

The archetype of the Moon beckons us to lean into our primal feelings. We must look under the hood and check the trunk before we take a road trip to the Sun. With the Moon, we have more visibility than the Star provided. But it's still very dark—we must combine our primal identities with the moonlight to navigate the way. Receptive moonlight merged with an innate sense of direction fuels our next adventure.

Before we expand our outer consciousness under the Sun, we have to explore under the hood and ensure that we're ready for the trip. The Moon card has us to drink tea with our subconscious, to intuitively identify and nurture the parts of ourselves that need healing. We have more light than starlight, but remember that it's still nighttime. So we pair the Moon's receptive light with our primal intuition to move us closer to the Sun's joy.

In a very outer-focused, Sun-driven world, the most visible parts of ourselves count as social currency. So the Moon card's call to return to our truest, most natural selves may seem very foreign in a culture where linear progress is what makes effort worthwhile. But we know that's not the case. We know that linearity is rare in the natural world. As we are a part of this ecosystem, we remember that we're not naturally equipped to live perfectly linear lives. Perhaps the biggest reminder of our most primal selves lies simply beyond our doors. Amongst flora and fauna, we find some of the most potent medicine available for healing and aligning our fragmented selves.

There's plenty of evidence that spending time in nature helps us reduce stress, heal, and improve our mental and physical health. This need to unwind in the wild became very apparent when COVID-19 struck and the trails quickly overcrowded. Understandably, all of us need an escape sometimes. Yet outdoor recreation is often less accessible for BIPOC, despite our knowledge that all of us can benefit from nature. Outdoor Afro has done a lot to reveal how common it is for Black people to report feeling excluded and unwelcome during outdoor excursions. There are so many stories from hikers of color about the racism they've experienced from white people on the trails.

Black people are some of the least likely folks in America to visit national parks, forests, and other wildernesses. White people constitute around 63 percent of the country's population, but make up from 88 to 95 percent of visitors to public outdoor land. The National Health Foundation shares:

> Racialized economic policies, employment discrimination, unequal access to quality education, and other fundamental tools that can build a person's economic standing have historically been denied to BIPOC communities; which makes camping, hiking or any similar ventures inaccessible. Costs of camping gear, entrance fees, lack of vacation days, unpaid leave, and other factors make it difficult for families to participate in outdoor recreation, particularly, BIPOC individuals who are more likely to face these economic barriers. However, even though access to capital reduces the likelihood of a person visiting a park or forest, the underlying issue to acknowledge is race.

In America, for example, there has been a long history of anti-Black racism in public spaces. In *Outside* magazine, Latria Graham describes white people's reaction to the creation of more public parks in the 1950s: "[It was an] escape from urban sprawl, at a time when urban was shorthand for blacks and immigrants." The exclusion continued through the National Park Service's outright exclusion of Black folks from bathrooms, picnic areas, and other areas throughout much of the twentieth century. This bleeds into the twenty-first century, as a 2011 NPS report exposes that three times as many Black people, compared to white people, feel too excluded and unsafe to frequent national parks.

And let's not get started on the pervasive racism within the past and present outdoor conservation movement.

Where do we even start? The National Health Foundation has a few good recommendations:

> To reverse the effects of racism on the outdoors, we must push for policies that have racial and spatial justice at the forefront. By using our social capital through spreading awareness and demanding greater accessibility to the natural world for all, we would be granting communities who have been historically separated from these spaces, an opportunity to enjoy them as well. Programs like Every Kid Outdoors strive to make the outdoors more inclusive by offering free or low-cost outdoor programs to children from low-income families. Community Nature Connection focuses on outdoor equity through access and exploration programs. Their Transit to Trails program offers free buses from low-income urban areas to natural spaces like beaches, national parks and mountains.

In addition to supporting organizations committed to environmentalism for all, we can also engage in active efforts to listen to BIPOC voices who share their experiences and knowledge so we can continue to mobilize through awareness and demanding greater accessibility to the natural world for all. In turn, we could open spaces to communities that have been historically displaced and removed so they can enjoy them without fear.

The Moon tells us that the wild is for everyone because it's within everyone. This is why we must turn our lens to increasing access to outdoor leisure—access to escape, rest, explore, and heal.

Part of dismantling systemic racism is removing what blocks our view of the moon. This means removing restricted access to the wild—internal and external—removing dangers and roadblocks in the path of healing, removing the obligation that many people have to stay on society's hamster wheel without a break. We peel back layers upon layers until we access the intrinsic, instinctual truth that we are all wild inside and the healing medicine of the outdoors belongs to everyone.

SUGGESTED EXERCISES

1. Read The Melanin Base Camp "Guide to Outdoor Allyship" and *Brown Gal Trekker*'s "Diversity, Equity & Inclusion: 26 Ways (& More) to Be an Ally in the Outdoor Industry"; then commit to some concrete ways that you will become a better ally to BIPOC in the outdoors. Then perform those actions.

2. Organize and/or support adventures that bring BIPOC—children and/or adults—to the outdoors.

3. Reach out to major outdoor brands, such as REI, and demand greater support for connecting BIPOC to nature.

4. Listen to the *Outside Voices* podcast. You might choose to begin with S1, Episode 4: "Finding Black Joy in the Outdoors" with Brittany Leavitt.

5. Watch the Outbound Collective's "Here We Stand" video (10 min, 31sec; captioned).

Identifying as the Moon Card

How do you already embody the Moon card? Use this list of words commonly associated with this card to identify the qualities that you do and don't want to work with as you help create a radically more equitable world.

■ Circle the qualities you already embody and can leverage as a superpower.

■ Draw a heart around the qualities you want to embody more deeply or frequently.

■ Draw a square around the qualities you want to transmute or avoid.

Introspective	Receptive	Insecure	Repressed instincts	Hidden agendas
Vigilant	Uncertain	Brave	Afraid of letting go	Creative
Good judgment	Hides	Psychic	Emotionally balanced	Superficial
Creative blocks	Concentration	Trust	Not knowing yourself	Forces what can't be forced

Affirmations for Embodying the Moon Archetype

As you follow the Moon's light, you might choose an affirmation to motivate you when the work is difficult. Affirmations can strengthen commitment by supporting your confidence in achieving personal and community goals. They can also help combat fear, anxiety, self-doubt, and loss of motivation, which are common feelings that come up in social justice work. You can chant them, write them down, meditate on them, add them to your phone background, or otherwise work with them consistently to keep focused on your objectives. Here are some examples.

"I'm brave enough to know myself."

"I listen to the call of the wild."

"I am ancestrally powered."

"My body speaks to me in creative ways."

"I am more than my anxiety."

 Often, the most powerful affirmations are the ones we create for ourselves. Take some time to jot down your personal affirmations.

Magical Practices to Conjure the Moon Card

Notice where you practice gratitude or indebtedness to colonizers. Stop suppressing aspects of your racialization, wherever safe. Identify the ways you seek white approval. Make amends for ancestors' harm. Explore what makes you uncomfortable in multiracial spaces. Train your intuition to notice casual racism. Confront the fact that unconscious bias is just as much a part of your identity as conscious values. Take a test to identify your biases. Unfriend TERFs. Address ways you consider certain groups monoliths. Ask yourself if there are certain types of people from racial groups that seem less safe or acceptable than others. Figure out your relationship with colorism. Trust your instincts about speaking up. Explore how racism showed up in your childhood. Protect Black mothers.

Becoming the Moon Archetype

Meditate on your relationship with the Moon, and use what you know to plan real-world action. By responding to these prompts, you are committing to doing the work—period.

SET A PERSONAL, RELATIONAL, OR COLLECTIVE INTENTION

✎ Name an objective that your work will center around.

✎ Plan specific actions for this objective that you will take as you embody the Moon card.

✎ This [day/week/month/event], I will embody the Moon card in my liberation work by _____

✎ This work is important because _____

✎ The affirmation I will repeat is _____

REFLECT ON YOUR EXPERIENCE

✎ Evolution is iterative and often nonlinear. As we pursue our goals, we must regularly evaluate our actions, mistakes, and learnings to inform the next cycles of change. Review your experience and identify what you can take with you as you move through your antiracism work.

- Successes

- Setbacks

- Frustrations

- Questions

- Other reflections

- Next steps

Advocate for Mental Health

The Moon dives within to strengthen their relationship with their interior. As such, this archetype can turn our focus toward mental health: Who gets diagnosed? Who deserves treatment? What are the risks of being a BIPOC with a mental illness? Why is mental health such a critical—and sometimes life-threatening—intersection for already marginalized people?

Use the following prompts to explore the relationship between mental health and structural racism:

1. What is Black joy?

2. What is racial trauma?

3. How does the mental burden of racism affect physical health?

4. What does wellness mean for different cultures in your local community?

5. How does mental illness disproportionately burden different racial groups?

6. How do socioeconomic disparities relate to mental illness? Why do some people get treatment, while others go to jail?

7. Define cultural competence in medical facilities and describe its impact.

8. Name ten common barriers to mental health care.

9. List five Black therapists in your community.

19

THE SUN

. . . there is more to Blackness than our struggle.

—ANGELA SHANTÉ

The Sun's far-reaching rays shine light on what it's like to exist authentically in the external world. The inner knowledge gained with the Moon flows into the Sun's outer integration. The Sun is a rebirth. Birth is a creation, and the Sun's reinventive energy asks us to create—authentically. This means tapping into our internal resources to create the things that only we can put out into the world. We've taken so many leaps; we've done so much introspection. We know the different parts of ourselves enough to amalgamate them into our own blend of energy, of magic, of creation. With the Sun, we bring our self-knowledge into the world through direct connection to our personal source energy. We don't hide our light at this point; we shine our distinctive warmth toward others.

The Sun asks: what makes you feel alive? This archetype reminds us that everything on our planet is a manifestation of solar energy. We have the sun to thank for everything in our lives. As such, we can turn to the Sun card for ways to become more conscious of the awe this world has to offer. When we open our hearts to awe, we create more space for wonder, joy, elation, and connection. The Sun is about truly engaging with life, celebrating the fact that we exist and have some control over where we focus our energies. This card asks us to be present, to energetically align our goals and actions. Saying yes to life can be a risk in itself. The Sun says: just do it, be alive, and feel all of the accessible senses that you encounter along the way.

The Sun illuminates our truest selves, the inner and the outer. Here we can see things as they really are, including that we are more capable when we show up as our most authentic selves (whenever safe). It's time to stop hiding our light.

All that work you've gone through so far? Be proud of it, because you're still here. Quit feeding your shame and stop blocking your energy from going where you genuinely want it to go. It's time to get honest about how we've suppressed our true selves and take time to align our inner truths with our external journey. Aligned energy is powerfully potent.

The Sun card isn't just about ourselves; it's also about all of us. Collectivity is a major theme, as every single person relies on the sun as the source of all life. Working with this archetype can help us celebrate our individuality and how it operates in concert with the interconnectedness of all things.

The Sun archetype can

- Express vibrant positivity and warmth
- Have a great sense of humor
- Celebrate others' successes publicly
- Own their sense of self
- Find opportunities for growth
- Feel comfortable in the spotlight
- Serve as a motivational speaker, party planner, farmworker, or child caretaker

Embodied Keywords

Pull out the Sun card from one deck or several. Take a deep breath and pause. Gaze at the imagery. From a liberation perspective, envision yourself in the card's landscape. Be the archetype. Name some keywords that you personally associate with this card. Remember, your definitions are more relevant to your tarot reading than what's in the little white book. Here are a few keywords to help get you started.

> Creativity, contentment, radiance, success, motivation, rebirth, family, communal living, inner child, abundance, fullness, breakthroughs, self-actualization, revived purpose, recognition, connection, wonder, source, aliveness, active energy, vitality, good fortune, growth, travel, movement

 Your keywords: _____

The Sun in Liberation Work

The Sun card embodies the popular saying "Joy is an act of resistance" and applies it in the most collective way in all of the tarot. Some may bristle at the quote, concerned that it simply palliates the guilt we feel when we are joyful in a world with dismal realities. Yet joy is different from willful ignorance. Joy gives strength and sustenance to social justice. And we are the deliverers.

The Sun's focus on collective consciousness combines with an emphasis on rejoicing to cultivate community among activists and benevolent troublemakers. Celebrations disrupt tension. Joy often lowers our defenses enough to connect—dance, sing, shout, drum—in ways that mentally and physically join us together. We lower the walls we've erected around ourselves to bond with each other over our shared successes and honor our movements' collage of individual skills and efforts. For example, laughs and camaraderie after a heated debate about antiracist strategy can relax agitation and conjure reunification. The Sun pays attention to opportunities for us to find commonalities and bond together in the fight toward true equity. A unified group can be hard to quell.

In "A Brief for the Defense," poet Jack Gilbert elaborates:

> If we deny our happiness, resist satisfaction, we lessen the importance of their deprivation. We must risk delight. We can do without pleasure, but not delight. Not enjoyment. We must have the stubbornness to accept our gladness in the ruthless furnace of this world. To make injustice the only measure of our attention is to praise the devil.

Communally focused, the Sun works to bring families together, such as the ones torn apart by border control and disjointed public family welfare services. The Sun builds, supports, and sustains systems that uplift healthy family programs and protect marginalized children. The Sun seeks to fix related structures such as substantiation decisions, interpretations of confidentiality statutes, central registries, mandated reporting, and how immigration impacts family welfare legislation.

The Sun combats gentrification and the many ways it disrupts local communities and overshadows cultural expressions and ways of life. They defend residents' abilities to express vibrancy and pride in who they are. The Sun takes notes from movements such as Washington D.C.'s defense of go-go music in the face of local colonialism.

As the Sun reminds us to shine our light upon others, this archetype commands that we share our abundant resources. We notice the ways that our cup runneth over. Then we share. We share our money: mutual aid. We share our time: devotion. We share our knowledge: education. We share viable job opportunities: financial elevation. We share about others' skills to people who need them: community. We have to bring justice to our pasts, but our priorities lie with the people living under the sun right now.

Correspondences for Inspiration

Consider exploring sources of inspiration that you associate with the Sun card. To help get you started, here are a few popular ones.

> Pepper, sandalwood, cloves, labdanum, frankincense, saffron, amber, cinnamon, sunstone, chrysolite, honey calcite, pyrite, gold, diamond, tiger's eye, hummingbirds, salamander, lion, peacock, snakes, yellow flowers, cypress, hazel, heliotrope, angelica, bay laurel, chamomile, dates, eucalyptus, ginseng, juniper, peony, citrus fruits, pineapples, sesame, sugarcane, chrysanthemum

✎ What reminds you of the Sun card? How do these things inspire you to keep going?

How the Sun Card Can Show Up

There are as many interpretations of tarot as there are people who have ever lived. There is no completely universal card interpretation because there is no completely universal perspective on life. Your and your clients' interpretations are what matter the most during a reading. Of all the possible magical ingredients, we humans are the most powerful in enacting real-world change. However, there are strong collective energies around the themes that appear more frequently when a particular archetype shows up. Here are some of those common motifs.

THE BALANCED SUN

- Attempts to be fully present
- Organizes communities
- Celebrates others' uniqueness
- Helps revitalize movements
- Offers creative solutions to collective issues
- Is unashamed to be themselves
- Centers collective liberation

✎ **My relationship to the Sun archetype feels balanced when** _____

THE IMBALANCED SUN

- Works from a myopic perspective
- Views joy as frivolous
- Lacks care for community
- Associates "light" with whiteness
- Operates on a scarcity mentality
- Has difficulty seeing their unique skills
- Is shortsighted

✎ **My relationship to the Sun archetype feels imbalanced when** _____

Black Joy and the Sun

In *Seventy-Eight Degrees of Wisdom,* Rachel Pollack writes of the Sun: "By accepting the Moon's fearful images, we bring the energy outside ourselves giving all of life a radiance." A new day is born and shines its light and warmth on us all—yes, all of us have the right to feel the sunlight, the right to feel alive. Doing the dirty work of healing provides us with more space for the possibility of joy. Here comes the sun.

LIFE / INTEGRATION / REBIRTH / EMBODIED AUTHENTICITY / INTERCONNECTEDNESS / COMMUNITY / UNIVERSAL CONSCIOUSNESS / CONTENTMENT / REGENERATION / INTERNAL RESOURCES / BRIGHTER VISION / CREATIVITY / ALIGNED ENERGY / SHAME RELEASED / CONFIDENCE / JOY / JOY / JOY

The sun itself may not belong to us, but the option to choose joy does. Yes, for each one of us. When the Sun card is reversed, the sun is still shining bright somewhere, even if you can't see it. Key nineteen has us adding one and nine to make ten, a symbol of wholeness and togetherness. At the number ten's detriment, we might find heavy burdens that block our view of the sun.

Anti-Black societies often politicize and police Black joy, aiming to sustain white privilege—including respectability politics. How many times have we heard of a white person calling the police on a predominately Black event simply because it was Black? (Remember Barbecue Becky?) Intentionally or not, some people see Black joy as distracting, suspicious, offensive, or dangerous. Yet this joy, relief, and community persist despite oppression, violence, and emotional burnout.

When Daunte Wright was murdered by police, many of us to wonder: when are we ever allowed to completely feel joy? For some people, April 11, 2021, was just another day. And for others, it was a painful reminder—a reminder that it can be extremely difficult for marginalized people to truly experience the sun's expanse, its optimism, its light upon a clear path ahead when generational trauma and white supremacist abuse and murder continue to threaten and harm our communities.

Yet Black joy persists.

In *The Tarot Handbook*, Angeles Arrien writes of the Sun card's creativity: "All creative processes are a form of play and exploration." When we meet the Sun card, we've journeyed to create more space for things like happiness that can radiate beyond ourselves. As such, the Sun card calls on us to use our creativity to generate more space for joy—an inherent right—in the world. It's not enough to just fight for justice; we must also fight for joy. Full stop.

How can you create more space for Black and Brown people to live more joyful, unapologetically expressive lives, without the threat of abuse? How can you create more space for others' joy? How can you connect with the value of joy through the lens of the Sun? And what does this mean for your antiracism work?

While you are envisioning ideal futures, marinate in this quote from writer Taylor K. Shaw:

> *I dance in the mirror. I wash my face twice a day. I kiss my partner gingerly at random times to show love to the divine in him and receive love for the divine in me. I am kind with the words I speak to myself and generous with rest. Through doing the work of healing traumas and honoring my purpose—to be light—I daily promise to soften my gaze on myself. That promise has changed everything for me as a Black woman. In moments like these, it is important to remember that our joy is a key ingredient of our freedom. Without practicing joy, we cannot truly be free. Just like our demands for justice, our joy must be nonnegotiable. I move away from the tropes of strength and perfection that have been pushed onto us and step into the understanding that perfect is holding the hand of the little girl inside me and letting her know that I love her and I will never stop looking to bring her joy. Being a Black woman in and of itself brings me joy.*

Now can be the time when you prioritize marginalized peoples' ability to feel the sun on their skin and to bask in exquisite, weightless joy.

SUGGESTED EXERCISES

1. Read firsthand reflections on what Black joy looks like in "Black Joy, We Deserve It" by Cody Charles.

2. Read Stacey Patton's "Even Black Joy Is a Crime."

3. Learn about the #DontMuteDC movement's story.

4. Watch "What Is #BlackBoyJoy and Why Do We Need It?" by The Root (1 min, 40 sec; captioned).

5. Learn about Afropunk!

6. Explore how Black women have built movements and cultivated joy.

7. Read "Black Joy Is Not a Crime" and "We Will Continue #laughingwhile black" by Altheria Gaston.

Identifying as the Sun Card

How do you already embody the Sun card? Use this list of words commonly associated with this card to identify the qualities that you do and don't want to work with as you help create a radically more equitable world.

- Circle the qualities you already embody and can leverage as a superpower.

- Draw a heart around the qualities you want to embody more deeply or frequently.

- Draw a square around the qualities you want to transmute or avoid.

Bold	Attention aligned with energy	Reparenting inner child	Internally resourced	Fear of trusting joy
Weary	Shameful	Loving	Denies silver linings	Regenerative
Endurance	Feels belonging in the world	Energetic	Egocentric	Shares their gifts freely
Only celebrates major milestones	Prioritizes pleasure	Presently conscious	Sensory	Disconnected from body

Affirmations for Embodying the Sun Archetype

As you soak in the Sun's rays, you might choose an affirmation to motivate you when the work is difficult. Affirmations can strengthen commitment by supporting your confidence in achieving personal and community goals. They can also help combat fear, anxiety, self-doubt, and loss of motivation, which are common feelings that come up in social justice work. You can chant them, write them down, meditate on them, add them to your phone background, or otherwise work with them consistently to keep focused on your objectives. Here are some examples.

"I am alive and I feel alive."

"My magic is more potent when I am authentic."

"My energy flows wherever my attention goes."

"I am joyfully accountable to myself."

"I am constantly coming into my own."

✎ Often, the most powerful affirmations are the ones we create for ourselves. Take some time to jot down your personal affirmations.

Magical Practices to Conjure the Sun Card

Defend marginalized children. Paint murals in your community. Offer free or sliding scale energy healing services. Plan community celebrations. Commit to a cause in a new way. Broadcast stories of oppression intentionally buried by oppressive forces. Travel to support protests that need greater force. Build more playgrounds and other recreational spaces. Meaningfully connect movements with similar objectives. Create a resource where people can see and reflect on organizational successes. Reveal truths about problematic public figures. Increase access to healthy foods. Make more space for different people in your organization to uniquely contribute.

Becoming the Sun Archetype

Meditate on your relationship with the Sun and use what you know to plan real-world action. By responding to these prompts, you are committing to doing the work—period.

SET A PERSONAL, RELATIONAL, OR COLLECTIVE INTENTION

✎ Name an objective that your work will center around.

✎ Plan specific actions for this objective that you will take as you embody the Sun card.

✎ This [day/week/month/event], I will embody the Sun card in my liberation work by

_____

✎ This work is important because _____

✎ The affirmation I will repeat is _____

REFLECT ON YOUR EXPERIENCE

✎ Evolution is iterative and often nonlinear. As we pursue our goals, we must regularly evaluate our actions, mistakes, and learnings to inform the next cycles of change. Review your experience and identify what you can take with you as you move through your antiracism work.

- Successes

- Setbacks

- Frustrations

- Questions

- Other reflections

- Next steps

Address Your Colorism

We see color because we have the Sun. Yet we've all heard the phrase, "I don't see color." The *Oxford English Dictionary* defines *colorism* as "prejudice or discrimination against individuals with a dark skin tone, typically amongst people of the same ethnic or racial group." Yet, it's so much more. Use the following prompts to explore what colorism is and how it impacts our everyday perspectives and interactions.

1. In your own words, what is colorism?

2. What is the history of colorism?

3. Who benefits from colorism?

4. Name some common myths about colorism.

5. How does colorism affect people around the world?

6. Outside of skin color, how do other physical traits play a role in colorism?

7. How does mass media reflect the reality of colorism? What are some examples?

8. How does social media perpetuate colorism? What are some examples?

9. Why do many people avoid the topic of colorism?

10. How does colorism show up in dating and marriage?

11. Name the difference between colorism and preference.

12. How does colorism influence or impact friendships?

13. How does colorism affect you?

14. What tools do you have to help counteract colorism in your inner circles and the greater collective?

20

JUDGEMENT

My humanity is bound up in yours,
for we can only be human together.

—DESMOND TUTU

At a crossroads, the Judgement card sounds a reverberating horn, awakening us to the undeniable news: it's time to begin a new stage of life. A new era is dawning, and Judgement asks us to apply the past to discern how we can live our lives in different ways. The key here is to view judging as discernment, rather than punitive evaluation. View your past self lovingly and gently. You did the best you could with what you had. Grant yourself an appropriate level of absolution. And now that you know better, so it's time to do better.

A time of Judgement is a time of reflection and self-evaluation, but this period is distinct from the introspection of the Hermit and Temperance cards. The Judgement card intentionally posits our reflections against the backdrop of the collective. Our evolution is society's evolution. When we think about ourselves and the work we've done, we consider who is judging us. We judge ourselves, but there are people to whom we want to show our authentic integrity. How might they view our progress? And how might they respond to it?

With self-reflection comes the dissolution of contracts that no longer serve ourselves and the collectives. We have to end what's expired in order to move forward. Some of the practices and narratives are holdovers from what our past selves needed. Discern what needs to go for the good of the world.

With discernment, the Judgement archetype trusts the internal and external signs they're sensing. At this point in the Major Arcana, we have done and seen so much and now we're gifted with the ability to make the most thoughtful decisions we possibly can. No matter how you feel about it, everything in your life has led you to this specific moment. There is an integrated collage of your journey thus far. Gaze upon it and ask: Where do I go from here? And how can I do it responsibly?

The Judgement archetype can

- Believe in and follow their callings
- Communicate very clearly and directly
- Transform themselves in ways that directly affect others
- Be keenly aware of their motivations and desires
- Balance intuition and intellect to make big decisions confidently
- Know when it's time to level up
- Be a paramedic, debt counselor, manager, or hiring specialist

Embodied Keywords

Pull out the Judgement card from one deck or several. Take a deep breath and pause. Gaze at the imagery. From a liberation perspective, envision yourself in the card's landscape. Be the archetype. Name some keywords that you personally associate with this card. Remember, your definitions are more relevant to your tarot reading than what's in the little white book. Here are a few keywords to help get you started.

Perception, rebirth, renaissance, self-evaluation, awakening, second chances, clearing, integrity, breaking habits, signs, research, purpose, reckoning, transition, reincarnation, absolution, destiny, redemption, decisiveness, underworld

✎ **Your keywords:** _____

The Judgement Card in Liberation Work

After moving through the highs and lows, the ebbs and flows of the Major Arcana so far, Judgement calls us to rise up to the undeniable occasion of reckoning like we've never reckoned before. We've courageously taken risks, learned lessons, dived deep into the interior and returned to the surface as integrated, fuller beings than we were when we leapt with the Fool. The penultimate major card has us take a straightforward, no BS look at today's reality to create more effective strategies in pursuit of equity and justice. A phase of Judgement is one that we can't ignore. The following card, the World, offers wholeness and fulfillment. But we don't arrive there before getting real about what the Sun revealed about who we truly are and what we've done. Judgement is an unmistakable call for self and community review.

Judgement meets us at a crossroads and reminds us of our volition. We can choose to stay still or to move toward a more liberated world. If we want a more ideal future, we can't sit idly by as the world turns. Often represented by Pluto, Judgement goes into the shadowy underworld to raise buried power, to bring core energy to the surface. As such, Judgement asks us to use our inner power to hold a mirror to all of the activism work we and our organizations have done so far—the good and the bad, the wins and the losses, things we are proud of and things we wish we'd done differently. We are a living amalgam of all we've done, and we have to own it all. We transcend into the World when we face the truth and commit to change. The stakes are high: Being a devoted, effective change-maker isn't just for ourselves, but also for our communities and the greater world. At the other end of Judgement is freedom.

So how can you reflect? How can you get your organization to reflect? One strategy is by holding an honest retrospective. Ask yourself the following questions:

What went well?

What didn't go well?

What was frustrating?

What questions do I still have?

Judgement is an opportunity to come clean and to move forward with honesty and respect for the people you are liberating. There's no such thing as a clean slate, but Judgement asks us to move forward as newer, more learned people. We devote ourselves to the present, and to our community's progress and renewal. Judgement is the turning point where we accept deeper responsibility, clearly informed by what we've done and what we're meant to do on this planet. We know our past and what we want to change. So how will we hold ourselves accountable?

Correspondences for Inspiration

Consider exploring sources of inspiration that you connect with the Judgement card. To help get you started, here are a few popular associations.

> Citrus fruits, nettle, hibiscus, warming spices, fire opal, brass, iron, malachite, porcupine, hedgehogs, sunflower, marigold, garlic, mustard seed, clocks, red poppy, Pluto, scrying tools

✎ **What reminds you of the Judgement card? How do these things inspire you to keep going?**

How the Judgement Card Can Show Up

There are as many interpretations of tarot as there are people who have ever lived. There is no completely universal card interpretation because there is no completely universal perspective on life. Your and your clients' interpretations are what matter the most during a reading. Of all the possible magical ingredients, we humans are the most powerful in enacting real-world change. However, there are strong collective energies around the themes that appear more frequently when a particular archetype shows up. Here are some of those common motifs.

THE BALANCED JUDGEMENT ARCHETYPE

- Knows when it's time to rise beyond for their community
- Shows great integrity

- Takes on new responsibilities
- Gives second chances
- Changes their habits when necessary
- Knows when something is a sign or a coincidence
- Chooses to evolve

✎ My relationship to the Judgement archetype feels balanced when _____

THE IMBALANCED JUDGEMENT ARCHETYPE

- Knows what they can and can't control
- Criticizes harshly
- Indulges their doubts and regrets
- Refuses to deal with consequences
- Prevents change
- Ignores clear signs
- Loathes themselves

✎ My relationship to the Judgement archetype feels imbalanced when _____

Reconciling Our Mistakes with the Judgement Card

Hark! The Judgement card arrives, calling us to wake up—to heed the call instead of the convenience of ignoring it. In reducing to the number two, key twenty can remind us of our High Priestess, the one who goes into the underworld and returns with what they've seen. As such, hanging out with the Judgement archetype can be a potent opportunity for us to look into ourselves, our underworld, and identify what we choose to return to the World with. This is a reconciliation point. This is where we follow the call to honestly evaluate ourselves so we can bring truth to light. When we reconcile our actions, feelings, and ideas, we prime ourselves to integrate our learnings and illuminations into how we carry ourselves in our evolving world.

Part of reconciliation involves noticing where we've gone wrong—and doing something about it.

When we do the critical work of self-reflection, we're more likely to notice instances where we've made mistakes. And yes, some of those mistakes may have caused harm. While we strive to do our work without causing damage to our communities, it's par for the course to err at some point.

But I'd imagine that very few of us like to be wrong.

Sometimes it's scary to even glance at where we've transgressed. Maybe we lied. Maybe we offended someone with a subtly racist comment. Maybe we unknowingly practiced gatekeeping. From realizing the damage we've caused, we can feel embarrassed, regretful, or tempted to flee relationships. We might fear losing respect, the consequences of external blame, or the loss of meaningful connections.

What if we owned up to our mistakes the way we expect public figures to do? What if, instead of running away from or glossing over the damage we've done, we used mistakes as opportunities to model the accountability that our ideal future needs to ethically sustain itself? Wouldn't the movement be even stronger and more unified if everyone practiced honest self-evaluation?

The work of dismantling systemic oppression will continue to require many, if not most, of us to engage in challenging conversations where our vulnerability shows. Maybe we do lose something in the process, and that's okay. Our micro self-work presents itself in the macro when we hold ourselves accountable for acknowledging and repairing the harm we've caused.

Make it a habit to practice compassionate honesty in self-reflection. Where do you see an opportunity to apologize for a mistake and the impact it had? It doesn't have to be related to race. This is just to get you practicing. Reflect, own up to your behavior, apologize thoughtfully, address the impact, and change your behavior. And then carry this attitude with you as you engage in an antiracist lifestyle. Like everyone else, you are going to mess up. What will you do about it?

Read one, some, or all of the pieces in Racial Equity Tools' list of resources for individual accountability and for organizational and community accountability. Then make a game plan for holding yourself and other people accountable for oppressive behavior. Do this activity with the knowledge that sometimes it can be extremely uncomfortable, but it's still worthwhile.

Identifying as the Judgement Card

How do you already embody the Judgement card? Use this list of words commonly associated with this card to identify the qualities that you do and don't want to work with as you help create a radically more equitable world.

- Circle the qualities you already embody and can leverage as a superpower.
- Draw a heart around the qualities you want to embody more deeply or frequently.
- Draw a square around the qualities you want to transmute or avoid.

Decisive	Collectively minded	Reckless	Clarifies	Shares news
Confronts mistakes	Cord-cutting	Preoccupied with regrets	Objective	Assertive
Alert	Rash	Endures tests	Afraid to end contracts	Recognizes turning points
Practical	Inner critic	Knows what they want	Considers the greatest good	Capable of change

Affirmations for Embodying the Judgement Archetype

When heeding Judgement's call to action, you might choose an affirmation to motivate you when the work is difficult. Affirmations can strengthen commitment by supporting your confidence in achieving personal and community goals. They can also help combat fear, anxiety, self-doubt, and loss of motivation, which are common feelings that come up in social justice work. You can chant them, write them down, meditate on them, add them to your phone background, or otherwise work with them consistently to keep focused on your objectives. Here are some examples.

"Endings conjure beginnings."

"My transformation is a gift to the world."

"I am more than my inner critic."

"My personal consciousness blends with the collective consciousness."

"I'm not afraid to look back."

✎ Often, the most powerful affirmations are the ones we create for ourselves. Take some time to jot down your personal affirmations.

Magical Practices to Conjure the Judgement Card

Define shared agendas for change. Know there's no such thing as a completely good or bad person. Read the room and ask who is making decisions for whom. Avoid weaponizing vulnerability. Stop making excuses for the ways you perpetuate oppression through words, actions, and upholding systems. Challenge defensiveness against major change. Practice generative conflict. Build a culture of feedback. Become willing to accept accountability. Deconstruct internalized white dominance. Notice when you're intellectualizing the struggle others experience daily. Notice where you feel personally attacked in antiracist spaces. Recognize your own limitations.

Becoming the Judgement Archetype

Meditate on your relationship with Judgement, and use what you know to plan real-world action. By responding to these prompts, you are committing to doing the work—period.

SET A PERSONAL, RELATIONAL, OR COLLECTIVE INTENTION

✎ Name an objective that your work will center around.

✎ Plan specific actions for this objective that you will take as you embody the Judgement card.

✎ This [day/week/month/event], I will embody the Judgement card in my liberation work by _____

✎ This work is important because _____

✎ The affirmation I will repeat is _____

REFLECT ON YOUR EXPERIENCE

✎ Evolution is iterative and often nonlinear. As we pursue our goals, we must regularly evaluate our actions, mistakes, and learnings to inform the next cycles of change. Review your experience and identify what you can take with you as you move through your antiracism work.

- Successes

- Setbacks

- Frustrations

- Questions

- Other reflections

- Next steps

Consider Cancel Culture

Judgement centers on reckoning with the truth and dealing with absolution. In cultures across the world, "canceling" manifests in different ways. The term "cancel culture" has risen in America in the last decade, raising questions of who gets canceled, as well as why and how. In often highly visible ways, cancellation intersects with racism in determining who stays canceled and who gets a shot at redemption. Research on cancel culture; then answer the following reflection questions.

1. What is cancel culture?

2. What can the process of cancellation involve?

3. What are some examples of people who have been canceled?

4. In popular media, how does cancel culture show up for different races?

5. How is cancel culture effective?

6. How is cancel culture ineffective?

7. What's the difference between "calling in" and "calling out"?

8. Imagine alternatives to cancel culture.

21

THE WORLD

What's in your soul is in your soul.

—WHITNEY HOUSTON

The World arrives at the end of the Major Arcana, but it tells us: all endings are also beginnings. Key twenty-one points to the sense of fulfillment that happens after we learn hard lessons and bring ourselves to accountability. This archetype asks us to make sense of it all, to integrate the lessons from the Fool's journey in micro and macro ways. The World asks: how does your everyday, mundane life align to your visions for the world's future? While there are integrative opportunities in every tarot card, the World most pointedly says that our own personal lives are never separate from the rest of creation. We're part of something bigger, and we have to live aligned to our missions through recognizing broader stories and contexts. This archetype often reminds us to understand the systems we exist in and how we fit into them. We've got enough experience to make greater contributions to the collective, but we remain humble enough to understand that we don't know everything. And so the cycle of learning, acknowledging, repairing, and reflecting goes on. This isn't a stopping point, but a prompt to use new freedoms to flow in the present moment, to exist with and through the worldly realm. Again, we don't know everything, but it's time for us to recognize that even though being in the world can be mysterious, we've learned enough lessons to get vulnerable again in the path toward liberation. We are simultaneously teachers and students.

Getting vulnerable with the World requires a level of confidence that enables us to notice and engage with whatever comes our way. Sometimes readers turn to the World to ask if they're on the "right" path; the answer is usually yes. The

World suggests that we hold on to our truths and trust our judgment. Wherever we go, we bring all of ourselves, whether we hide it or broadcast it. Part of knowing ourselves is knowing and honoring our lineages. The World lays a solid foundation for reflecting on who and what helped us learn the deep lessons of the Major Arcana and then making sure to name them publicly to transfer knowledge more broadly. We didn't get here only by ourselves—we are individuals, but our humanness indicates that we've never been truly alone.

As key twenty-one, the World can speak to cycles ending, particularly ones that have deeply impacted ourselves and our communities. With this card comes culminations, breakthroughs, and achievements. This card often lets us know that we've come full circle, or that we're almost there. Yet the World is a dynamic figure, telling us that opportunity awaits and it's best we get curious. Illuminated in Saturn conjunct Jupiter, we see Saturn's focus on earthly work and concentration meet Jupiter's nucleus of higher thinking. This combination shows what's possible when we do the everyday work to raise our personal and collective consciousness. We give to and receive from the world. We invoke and evoke energy. We draw down and give back. We are constantly moving. Nothing's promised but change. At the end of the road is always another road, even if it hasn't yet been paved.

The World archetype can

- See tasks through to the end
- Show optimism
- Be tenacious
- Demonstrate awareness of global issues
- Have a fresh outlook
- Consciously uncouple themselves from others
- Be a scholar, cleaner, travel photographer, or flight attendant

Embodied Keywords

Pull out the World card from one deck or several. Take a deep breath and pause. Gaze at the imagery. From a liberation perspective, envision yourself in the card's landscape. Be the archetype. Name some keywords that you personally associate with this card. Remember, your definitions are more relevant to your tarot reading than what's in the little white book. Here are a few keywords to help get you started.

> Success, endings as beginnings, cycles, wrap-ups, archival, completion, integration, travel, closure, wholeness, dynamism, complexity, ease, humor, possibility, collective consciousness, infinity, interconnectedness, motion, potential, community, feeling of belonging, harmony, unity, reward, new outlook

✎ Your keywords: _____

The World Card in Liberation Work

The World is a permission slip to celebrate our accomplishments. Humbly, we recognize how much we've grown and achieved through love, community, consistency, flexibility, and teachability. Recognizing our growth can make us excited and curious about our next growth cycle.

Or we might just feel tired.

The World reflects fullness, and sometimes we are simply full of exhaustion. Challenging the power of white supremacy isn't easy, but we give the struggle all we can. The work is so urgent that we may forget to grant ourselves kindness, gratitude, grace, rest, recreation, and space. The world needs more of these things. Because we are of the world, so do we.

What makes us susceptible to activist burnout? In "'Frayed All Over': The Causes and Consequences of Activist Burnout Among Social Justice Education Activists," Paul C. Gorski and Cher Chen name a few examples: deep commitment, emotional investment, and the "burden of knowledge that society as a whole is unable or unwilling to face." Cultures of selflessness can exacerbate stress, as they can influence people to ignore, deny, and suppress their feelings. In "'Anger

Is Why We're All Here': Mobilizing and Managing Emotions in a Professional Activist Organization," Kathleen Rodgers states,

> The ubiquitous discourse of selflessness pervades the internal dynamics of the organization, and in terms of the emotional culture of the organization, it means that displays of personal strain, sadness, or depression, while perhaps understandable, are viewed by a considerable amount of the staff as unnecessary and self-indulgent.

Many of us have experienced the effects of stress. The American Psychological Association names several in "How Stress Affects Your Health": anxiety, depression, gastrointestinal problems, impaired memory and concentration, muscle pain, sleep disruption, increased risk of coronary disease—the list goes on.

Fatigue is not a badge of honor. It's a sign to check in. You can tell if you're burned out if you're feeling cynical, ineffective, or always tired. If this sounds resonant right now, you ought to rest. It's not just for you; burnout decelerates movements. We accomplish more when we take care of ourselves. Think about the difference between a day after a good night's sleep and a day after an all-nighter. Our work requires our energy.

SUGGESTED EXERCISE

Create a literal or digital care package for yourself with things that can soothe or delight you when you're feeling stretched. Keep it in a place you'll remember and don't hesitate to reach for it when you need it.

Correspondences for Inspiration

Consider exploring sources of inspiration that you associate with the World card. To help get you started, here are a few popular correspondences.

Pepperwort, odiferous roots, musk, sulfur, asafoetida, lead, onyx, hematite, lapis lazuli, golden marcasite, black opal, snake, toad, nocturnal animals, flies, carrion birds, black animals, common basilisk, oleander, patchouli, poplar, rye, nightshade, rue, morning glory, mosses, ivy, hemlock, comfrey, fern, yew, beet, cypress, belladonna

✎ What reminds you of the World card? How do these things inspire you to keep going?

How the World Card Can Show Up

There are as many interpretations of tarot as there are people who have ever lived. There is no completely universal card interpretation because there is no completely universal perspective on life. Your and your clients' interpretations are what matter the most during a reading. Of all the possible magical ingredients, we humans are the most powerful in enacting real-world change. However, there are strong collective energies around the themes that appear more frequently when a particular archetype shows up. Here are some of those common motifs.

THE BALANCED WORLD ARCHETYPE

- Commits to exploration
- Persists to the end, when possible and reasonable
- Works creatively with their limitations
- Acknowledges their teachers
- Shows gratitude
- Validates others' successes
- Is eager for new opportunities

✎ My relationship to the World archetype feels balanced when _____

THE IMBALANCED WORLD ARCHETYPE

- Lacks belief in oneself
- Gives up easily
- Is stubborn
- Fears the unknown
- Repeats patterns without learning from them
- Doesn't show up for themselves
- Struggles to recognize accomplishments

✎ My relationship to the World archetype feels imbalanced when _____

Cyclical Integration with the World Card

Even though we've been working with the Major Arcana with a focused lens, the World reminds us to avoid getting married to that lens. We can't afford for folks to refuse flexibility in a world that is continually shifting.

At this point, we've thought a lot about how we've done and how we do antiracism work in our everyday lives. Great, what's next? Evolution is the way of the world and, accordingly, so must be our work.

The work of untangling internalized racism and dismantling external, structural racism is supposed to feel hard, messy, and inconvenient. If your practice feels easy, straightforward, and convenient instead, you're probably due for an upgrade.

We can't do the same thing over and over again and expect different results. We've got to go deeper. We've got to go into the internal, like the High Priestess. We need sustainable and scalable structures that are equitable and community-driven, like the Emperor. We need to make space for joy, like the Sun. And maybe most importantly, we've got to just dive in, just like the Fool.

The World can remind us that everything we do is political, whether we like it or not. Here, we reflect, integrate, and commit to getting dirty all over again.

A better future is possible. I know this is true.

SUGGESTED EXERCISES

Reflect on your work, self-reflections, and learnings thus far. If everyone did what you've done, would your community be a better place? How could your work expand? How can you check in with yourself to make sure you haven't gotten too comfortable?

Answer the following:

- What will you do to get more uncomfortable in your everyday routine?

- What will you do to get more uncomfortable in your relationships?

- What will you do to get more uncomfortable in your community?

- What will you do to get more uncomfortable in your spiritual practice and/or services?

Now put the beginner's hat back on. Deeper in we go!

Identifying as the World Card

How do you already embody the World card? Use this list of words commonly associated with this card to identify the qualities that you do and don't want to work with as you help create a radically more equitable world.

- Circle the qualities you already embody and can leverage as a superpower.

- Draw a heart around the qualities you want to embody more deeply or frequently.

- Draw a square around the qualities you want to transmute or avoid.

Welcomes change	Resists mystery	Acknowledges their gifts	Vulnerable	Learns from mistakes
Apathetic	Toxic expectations	Knows they've always been whole	Persistent	Collects inspiration
Tenacious	Views life to be sacred	Takes the easy route	Embraces life fully	Takes quickest route
Easily defeated	Requires clear-cut closure	Knows when to reenergize	Cheers others on	Loses focus

Affirmations for Embodying the World Archetype

Stepping into the promising vastness of the World card, you might choose an affirmation to motivate you when the work is difficult. Affirmations can strengthen commitment by supporting your confidence in achieving personal and community goals. They can also help combat fear, anxiety, self-doubt, and loss of motivation, which are common feelings that come up in social justice work. You can chant them, write them down, meditate on them, add them to your phone background, or otherwise work with them consistently to keep focused on your objectives. Here are some examples.

"Everything is a spell." (quoted from Angela Mary Magick)

"The only true guarantee is change."

"I am strong when I live in my truth."

"I am the teacher and the student at the same time."

"I commit to the mystery."

✎ Often, the most powerful affirmations are the ones we create for ourselves. Take some time to jot down your personal affirmations.

Magical Practices to Conjure the World Card

Show up. Be present. Share your lessons. Live your lessons. Thank your teachers. Give land back. Get ready to get uncomfortable again. Dive back in.

Becoming the World Archetype

Meditate on your relationship with the World and use what you know to plan real-world action. By responding to these prompts, you are committing to doing the work—period.

SET A PERSONAL, RELATIONAL, OR COLLECTIVE INTENTION

✎ Name an objective that your work will center around.

✎ Plan specific actions for this objective that you will take as you embody the World card.

✎ This [day/week/month/event], I will embody the World card in my liberation work by _____

✎ This work is important because _____

✎ The affirmation I will repeat is _____

REFLECT ON YOUR EXPERIENCE

✎ Evolution is iterative and often nonlinear. As we pursue our goals, we must regularly evaluate our actions, mistakes, and learnings to inform the next cycles of change. Review your experience and identify what you can take with you as you move through your antiracism work.

- Successes
- Setbacks
- Frustrations
- Questions
- Other reflections
- Next steps

BUILDING A TOOLKIT

Talk the Talk

At the core of the World is the reality that we are of the world and in the world. We are never separate from the infinite ways we humans interconnect through everyday living. This archetype takes their lessons and expands the scope of their impact by communicating them with others. At the end of the Major Arcana, take some time to jot down the five toughest questions you've had to confront. Then plan to discuss each question with a unique person in your life. Ideally, these conversations happen in real time, in person or through video chat. Remember the person you were when you had to answer these questions and use empathy to create the space to have conversations on tough topics. Remember, your learnings mean nothing to the world if they never show up in it. You are the vessel.

Question: _____

I will discuss this with: _____

Notes from conversation: _____

Next steps we will take: _____

Question: _____

I will discuss this with: _____

Notes from conversation: _____

Next steps we will take: _____

Question: _____

I will discuss this with: _____

Notes from conversation: _____

Next steps we will take: _____

Question: _____

I will discuss this with: _____

Notes from conversation: _____

Next steps we will take: _____

Question: _____

I will discuss this with: _____

Notes from conversation: _____

Next steps we will take: _____

REFERENCES AND RESOURCES

2 The High Priestess

Dr. Kira Hudson Banks, "Reframing Internalized Racial Oppression: Shifting Our Theory of Oppression," (3:42 min) *Raising Equity*, YouTube, February 18, 2018.

Project Implicit, How We Think About Race/Ethnicity test, *projectimplicit.net*.

Beverly Daniel Tatum, *Why Are All the Black Kids Sitting Together in the Cafeteria? And Other Conversations About Race*, Basic Books, 2017.

3 The Empress

Hannah Eko, "As a Black Woman, I'm Tired of Having to Prove My Womanhood," BuzzFeed.News, February 27, 2018.

Rebecca Epstein, Jamilia Blake, and Thalia González, *Girlhood Interrupted: The Erasure of Black Girls' Childhood*, Georgetown Law Center on Poverty and Inequality, ebook 2017.

Rachel Pollack, *Seventy-Eight Degrees of Wisdom: A Tarot Journey to Self-Awareness*, Weiser Books, 3rd ed. rev., March 1, 2019.

4 The Emperor

Conscious Style Guide, *consciousstyleguide.com*.

Paul Laurence Dunbar, "Sympathy by Paul Dunbar," Poetry Foundation.

Audre Lorde, "The Master's Tools Will Never Dismantle the Master's House," in *Sister Outsider: Essays and Speeches*, Crossing Press, 2007.

Toni Morrison, *The Origin of Others*, Harvard University Press, 2017.

John A. Powell and Stephen Menendian, "The Problem of Othering: Towards Inclusiveness and Belonging," *Othering & Belonging*, June 29. 2017.

5 The Hierophant

Angeles Arrien, *The Tarot Handbook: Practical Applications of Ancient Visual Symbols*, Jeremy P. Tarcher/Putnam, 1997.

Nicole Ellis and Maya Lin Sugarman, "Why You Need to Keep Talking About Race with Your White Family," The Lily.

"Examples of Racial Microaggressions" list, UMN, *sph.umn.edu*.

Rebecca Hains, "Dear Fellow White People: Here's What to Do When You're Called Racist," *Washington Post*, August 23, 2019.

Tania Israel, *Beyond Your Bubble: How to Connect Across the Political Divide, Skills and Strategies for Conversations That Work*, APA LifeTools, August 11, 2020.

Sarah McCammon, "Want to Have Better Conversations About Racism with Your Parents? Here's How," NPR, June 15, 2020.

6 The Lovers

Ta-Nehisi Coates, "The Case for Reparations," *Atlantic*, June 15, 2014.

"Kimberlé Crenshaw on Intersectionality, More Than Two Decades Later" interview with Columbia Law School on June 8, 2017.

Sytonia Reid and Mary Meade, "6 Reasons to Support Black-Owned Businesses," Green America, updated February 2023; *www.greenamerica.org*.

7 The Chariot

Kat Blaque, "The History of Whiteness," YouTube, February 3, 2016.

Austin Channing Brown, "White Privilege Weariness" and "White Privilege Weariness Part 2," *Austin Channing Brown* blog, March 24, 2013, and April 1, 2014.

Ijeoma Oluo, "Confronting Racism Is Not About the Needs and Feelings of White People," *Guardian*, March 28, 2019.

Jonathan Osler, "Opportunities for White People in the Fight for Racial Justice," White Accomplices.

Pierleone Porcu, Daniela Carmignani, Wolfi Landstreicher, and Killing King Abacus, *Revolutionary Solidarity* (pamphlet), Elephant Editions, 2000.

Alexandria Villaseñor quoted in Fahys, Judy, et al, "There Is No Climate Justice Without Racial Justice," *Yes!* June 12, 2020, *yesmagazine.org*.

8 Strength

Morten Fibieger Byskov, "Focusing on How Individuals Can Stop Climate Change Is Very Convenient for Corporations," *Fast Company*, January 11, 2019.

Tess McClure, "Dark Crystals: The Brutal Reality Behind a Booming Wellness Craze," *Guardian*, September 17, 2019.

Moms Clean Air Force, "Climate Change in the African American Community" fact sheet, from the "What You Can Do About Climate Change" section.

Eva Wiseman, "Are Crystals the New Blood Diamonds?" *Guardian*, June 16, 2019.

9 The Hermit

Arlie Russell Hochschild, *The Managed Heart: Commercialization of Human Feeling*, University of California Press, March 2012.

Monica Johnson, "The Emotional Cost of Being a Black Woman in America" (16 min), TEDx Talks, YouTube.

Threads of Solidarity, "How to Compensate Black Women and Femmes on Social Media for Their Emotional Labor," February 26, 2018.

10 The Wheel of Fortune

Keri Gray, "Disability Is Intersectional" (captioned, 1 min), YouTube, July 9, 2020.

Sins Invalid, "10 Principles of Disability Justice," September 17, 2015.

Vilissa Thompson, "Black Disabled Woman Syllabus: A Compilation," Ramp Your Voice, May 2016.

11 Justice

Charisse Burden-Stelly, "Modern U.S. Racial Capitalism," *Monthly Review*, July 1, 2020.

Angela Davis, "We Can't Eradicate Racism Without Eradicating Racial Capitalism" (2 min, 35 sec; captioned), *Democracy Now!*, YouTube, June 14, 2020.

Karl Marx, *Poverty of Philosophy*, Twentieth Century Press of London, 1900.

Rachel Pollack, *Seventy-Eight Degrees of Wisdom: A Tarot Journey to Self-Awareness*, Weiser Books, 3rd ed. rev., March 1, 2019.

Rashawn Ray and Andre M. Perry, "Why We Need Reparations for Black Americans," Brookings Institute, April 15, 2020.

Olúfémi O. Táiwò and Liam Kofi Bright, "A Response to Michael Walzer," *Dissent*, August 7, 2020.

Kwame Ture and Charles V. Hamilton, "White Power: The Colonial Situation," in *Black Power: The Politics of Liberation*, Random House, 2011.

Eric Williams, *Capitalism and Slavery*, University of North Carolina Press, 1994.

Julia Carrie Wong, "What Picketing Taught Me About Feminism," *Salon*, August 16, 2013.

12 The Hanged One

Mapping Police Violence, *mappingpoliceviolence.org*.

13 Death

Dusty Bunker and Faith Javane, *Numerology and the Divine Triangle*, Para Research, 1979.

Fabian Luis Fernandez, "Hands Up: A Systematized Review of Policing Sex Workers in the U.S." dissertation, Yale University, 2016.

Erin Fitzgerald, Sarah Elspeth Patterson, Darby Hickey, Cherno Biko, and Harper Jean Tobin, *Meaningful Work: Transgender Experiences in the Sex Trade*, National Center for Transgender Equality, 2015.

Juniper Fitzgerald, "White Feminism, White Supremacy, White Sex Workers," Tits and Sass, March 22, 2017.

Melissa Grant, "The NYPD Arrests Women for Who They Are and Where They Go—Now They're Fighting Back," *Village Voice*, November, 22, 2016.

Juno Mac and Molly Smith, *Revolting Prostitutes: The Fight for Sex Workers' Rights*, Verso, 2018.

Rights Not Rescue: How to Be a Meaningful Ally to Sex Workers (brochure), SWOP-USA, February 2019.

Jasmine Sankofa, "From Margin to Center: Sex Work Decriminalization Is a Racial Justice Issue," Amnesty International website.

14 Temperance

Black Art in America, *www.blackartinamerica.com*.

Bottom of the Map podcast episodes.

Angie Jaime, "The 'Art World' Can't Exist in a Decolonized Future," *Teen Vogue*, June 20, 2020.

T. V. Reed, *The Art of Protest: Culture and Activism from the Civil Rights Movement to the Streets of Seattle*, University of Minnesota Press, 2nd ed., 2019.

Shantay Robinson, "Why Is Black Portraiture So Popular Today?" *Black Art in America*, August 21, 2022.

Antwaun Sargent, *The New Black Vanguard: Photography Between Art and Fashion*, Aperture, 2019.

Smithsonian American Art Museum, "African American Art: Harlem Renaissance, Civil Rights Era, and Beyond" slideshow, hosted on Google Arts & Culture.

15 The Devil

AfroPoets, *www.afropoets.net*.

Rachel Cargle, "When Feminism Is White Supremacy in Heels" *Harper's Bazaar*, August 16, 2018.

Open Road Media, "Honoring the Storytelling Tradition" (1.5 min, captioned), YouTube, February 8, 2012.

TMI Project's podcast, season two themed "Black Stories Matter."

16 The Tower

Dan Berger, Mariame Kaba, and David Stein, "What Abolitionists Do," *Jacobin*, August 24, 2017.

Gina Crosley-Corcoran, "Explaining White Privilege to a Broke White Person," Duke Medical School website, February 2022.

Ava DuVernay, *13th* (full feature, 1h 40 min, captioned), Kandoo Films; distributed by Netflix.

Rose Hackman, "'We Need Co-Conspirators, Not Allies: How White Americans Can Fight Racism," *Guardian*, June 26, 2015.

Ibram X. Kendi, *How to Be an Antiracist*, One World, 2019.

Violet Rush, "Owning the Role of White Co-Conspirator," *If/When/How*, August 8, 2017, quoted in MJ Knittel, "Making the Transition from Ally to Co-Conspirator," *Medium*, May 13, 2018.

Amanda Seales, "Side Effects of White Women," *Small Doses: Potent Truths for Everyday Use*.

What Did We Learn? with Alicia Garza and Wyatt Cenac, episode 57, October 5, 2017, Earwolf.

17 The Star

"Breaking Schools' Rules: A Statewide Study on How School Discipline Relates to Students' Success and Juvenile Justice Involvement," CSG Justice Center, July 2011.

Janine Francois, "Reparations for Black People Should Include Rest," *Vice*, January 7, 2019.

Natasha Marin, ed., *Black Imagination: Black Voices on Black Futures*, McSweeney's, February 4, 2020.

Benjamin Reiss, "Op-Ed: African Americans Don't Sleep as Well as Whites, an Inequality Stretching Back to Slavery," *Los Angeles Times*, April 23, 2017.

The Sleep Foundation, *www.sleepfoundation.org*.

18 The Moon

"Diversity, Equity & Inclusion: 26 Ways (& More) to Be an Ally in the Outdoor Industry," *Brown Gal Trekker*, November 11, 2018.

"Finding Black Joy in the Outdoors" with Brittany Leavitt, *Outside Voices* podcast S1, Episode 4.

Latria Graham, "We're Here. You Just Don't See Us," *Outside*, May 1, 2018.

Naomi Humphrey, "Breaking Down the Lack of Diversity in Outdoor Spaces," National Health Foundation website, July 20, 2020.

Outbound Collective, "Here We Stand" (10 min, 31 sec; captioned), YouTube, February 26, 2020.

Outdoor Afro, *outdoorafro.com*.

Danielle Williams, "Guide to Outdoor Allyship," The Melanin Base Camp, July 7, 2019.

19 The Sun

Angeles Arrien, *The Tarot Handbook: Practical Applications of Ancient Visual Symbols*, Jeremy P. Tarcher/Putnam, 1997.

Brea Baker, "For Black Women, Joy Is Nonnegotiable," *Elle*, July 2, 2020.

Cody Charles, "Black Joy, We Deserve It," *Medium*, February 17, 2017.

Altheria Gaston, "Black Joy Is Not a Crime and We Will Continue #laughingwhileblack," For Harriet, August 27, 2015.

Jack Gilbert, "A Brief for the Defense," from *Refusing Heaven: Poems by Jack Gilbert*, Knopf, 2007.

Stacey Patton, "Even Black Joy Is a Crime," *Dame Magazine*, June 8, 2015.

Rachel Pollack, *Seventy-Eight Degrees of Wisdom: A Tarot Journey to Self-Awareness*, Weiser Books, 3rd ed. rev., March 1, 2019.

The Root, "What Is #BlackBoyJoy and Why Do We Need It?" (1 min, 40 sec; captioned), April 10, 2017.

20 Judgement

Racial Equity Tools, "Accountability," *racialequitytools.org*.

21 The World

American Psychological Association, "How Stress Affects Your Health," *APA.org*, January 1, 2013.

Paul C. Gorski and Cher Chen, "'Frayed All Over': The Causes and Consequences of Activist Burnout Among Social Justice Education Activists," *Educational Studies* 51(5): 385–405.

Angela Mary Magick, *angelamarymagick.com*.

Kathleen Rodgers, "'Anger Is Why We're All Here': Mobilizing and Managing Emotions in a Professional Activist Organization," *Social Movement Studies* 9 (3): 273–92.

ABOUT THE AUTHOR

Maria Minnis is an unapologetically Black writer, artist, ritual facilitator, and tarot reader who teaches people about blending their spirituality with liberation work and sensuality. She has creatively worked with tarot for over twenty years and considers herself an eternal student of life and thus, the tarot. Her work is inspired by her belief that the end result of all magic should be to cultivate a more equitable and empathetic planet. Maria is the author of the blog series *Antiracism with the Tarot*. She holds a master of science degree in interactive media design from Quinnipiac University and a bachelor of arts degree in writing from James Madison University. She lives in Los Angeles with her life partner and their naked cat. Maria enthusiastically drinks from the flowing fire hose of life and wouldn't have it any other way. Visit her at *mariaminnis.com* and on Instagram @feminnis.

TO OUR READERS